COMPANIONS *in Christ*
A SMALL-GROUP EXPERIENCE IN SPIRITUAL FORMATION

The Way of SCRIPTURE

Participant's Book

M. Robert Mulholland Jr.
with Marjorie J. Thompson

UPPER ROOM BOOKS®
NASHVILLE

COMPANIONS IN CHRIST: THE WAY OF SCRIPTURE
Participant's Book
Copyright © 2010 by Upper Room Books®
All rights reserved.

The Upper Room® Web site http://www.upperroom.org

At the time of publication all Web sites referenced in this book were valid. However, due to the fluid nature of the Internet. some addresses may have changed or the content may no longer be relevant.

Unless otherwise stated, scripture quotations are the translation of M. Robert Mulholland Jr.

Scripture noted NRSV is taken from the New Revised Standard Version Bible, copyright © 1989 by the Division of Christian Education of the National Council of the Churches of Christ in the U.S.A. Used by permission. All rights reserved.

In referencing New Testament books where authorship is questioned by scholars, traditional attributions of authorship will be used.

Cover design: Left Coast Design, Portland, Oregon

Cover photo: Chris Thomaidis; Stone collection

Interior icon development: Michael C. McGuire, settingPace

First printing: 2010

Library of Congress Cataloging-in-Publication Data

Mulholland, M. Robert.
   The way of Scripture. Participant's book / M. Robert Mulholland Jr. with Marjorie J. Thompson.
     p. cm.
   ISBN 978-0-8358-1034-0
   1. Bible—Devotional use—Textbooks. 2. Bible—Reading.—Textbooks. I. Thompson, Marjorie J., 1953–
II. Thompson, Marjorie J., 1953– Way of Scripture. III. Title.
   BS617.8.T46 2010
   220.071—dc22   2010020389

Printed in the United States of America

**For more information on *Companions in Christ*
call 800-972-0433 or visit www.CompanionsInChrist.org**

Contents

Acknowledgments

The foundational twenty-eight-week program *Companions in Christ* grew from seeds of a vision long held by Stephen D. Bryant, publisher of Upper Room Ministries from 1997 to 2009. The vision took shape under the guidance of Marjorie J. Thompson, Director of Upper Room's Pathways in Congregational Spirituality and Spiritual Director to Companions in Christ from 1996 until early 2009. The vision quickly expanded into the adult Companions in Christ series, realized through the efforts of many people over the past eight years. Original advisers, consultants, authors, editors, and test churches are acknowledged in the foundational resource. We continue to be grateful for each person and congregation named there.

M. Robert Mulholland Jr. wrote the chapters in this Participant's Book. The daily exercises are the work of Marjorie J. Thompson, who also wrote *The Way of Scripture* Leader's Guide. Consultants included Mary Lou Redding, Eli Fisher, and Tony Peterson. Special thanks also go to our three test group leaders and their small groups who offered valuable feedback and insights into the development of the material: John Anderson, Trinity Presbyterian Church, Arvada, Colorado; Sandi Evans Rogers, Frederick Church of the Brethren, Frederick, Maryland; and Scott McBroom, Providence Baptist Church, Charleston, South Carolina.

Introduction

Welcome to *Companions in Christ: The Way of Scripture*, a small-group resource designed to help you explore the nature of scripture and the ancient, time-tested practice of *lectio divina*. This is not a Bible study, nor is it designed for persons new to Christian faith who may need good Bible study to provide a solid foundation for newly gained beliefs. Rather, *The Way of Scripture* is intended for committed Christians who are serious about adventuring into greater spiritual depths with God's Word.

In response to small groups who want to continue their exploration of spiritual practices that began with the original twenty-eight-week *Companions in Christ* resource, The Upper Room is developing the Companions in Christ series. *The Way of Scripture* is the ninth title and offers a seven-week journey (plus a preparatory meeting) of exploring perspectives and practices that engage us in spiritual formation with scripture.

Each resource in the Companions series expands on the foundational content in the twenty-eight-week resource and is presented in the same basic format. In the foundational resource, we explored the Christian spiritual life under five headings: Journey, Scripture, Prayer, Call (or vocation), and Spiritual Guidance. Additional volumes of the Companions series explore in greater depth one of these categories of practice.

The Way of Scripture falls under the general heading of Scripture. To explore this subject, we will engage the Bible with mind and heart, drawing on classic practices of scriptural meditation, prayer, and journaling. It is important to underscore that this resource is *not* a Bible study in any conventional sense. It offers a formational approach to scripture that can complement and deepen traditional Bible study.

Like the foundational *Companions in Christ* resource, *The Way of Scripture* will help you deepen essential practices of the Christian life. It focuses on your daily experience of God and your growing capacity to respond to grace with gratitude, trust, love, and self-offering. Because this exploration takes place in the midst of a small group, you can expect increasingly to realize the blessings of mutual support, encouragement, guidance, and accountability in Christian community. Your growth in faith and maturation in spirit will benefit your congregation or faith community as well.

About the Resource and Process

Like all *Companions* resources, *The Way of Scripture* has two primary components: first, individual reading and daily exercises throughout the week with this Participant's Book; and, second, a weekly two-hour meeting based on directions in the Leader's Guide.

Each weekly chapter in the Participant's Book introduces new material and provides five daily exercises to help you reflect on your life in light of the chapter content. After the Preparatory Meeting of your group, you will begin a weekly cycle as follows: On day 1 you will be asked to read the chapter; on days 2–6 you will complete each of the five daily exercises (found at the end of each week's reading); on day 7 you will meet with your group.

The daily exercises aim to help you move from information (knowledge *about*) to experience (knowledge *of*). The time commitment for one daily exercise is twenty to thirty minutes. An important part of this process involves keeping a personal notebook or journal in which you record reflections, prayers, and questions for later review and for reference at the weekly group meeting.

Weekly meetings include time for sharing reflections on the exercises of the past week and for moving deeper into the content of the chapter through various learning and prayer experiences. Meetings begin and end with simple worship times. You will need to bring your Participant's Book, your Bible, and your personal notebook or journal to each weekly group meeting.

The Companions in Christ Web Site

Another dimension of resources in the Companions in Christ series is the Web site. The Companions in Christ Web site is designed to provide information on the entire Companions family of resources (children, youth, and adults). The site offers helpful information for leaders, group members, and those desiring more information about involvement in Companions. Visit www.CompanionsInChrist.org.

Your Personal Notebook or Journal

Keeping a journal or personal notebook (commonly called journaling) will be one of the most important dimensions of your personal experience with *Companions in Christ: The Way of Scripture*. The Participant's Book gives you daily spiritual exercises each week. More often than not, you will be asked to note your thoughts, reflections, questions, feelings, or prayers in relation to the exercise.

You may find that this kind of personal writing quickly becomes second nature despite your inexperience. Your thoughts may start to pour out of you, giving expression to an inner life that has never been released. If, however, you find the writing difficult or cumbersome, give yourself permission to try it in a new way. Because a journal is for your eyes only, you may choose any style that suits you. You need not worry about making your words sound beautiful or about writing with correct grammar and spelling. You don't even need to write complete sentences. Jotting down key ideas, insights, or musings in a few words or phrases works just fine. You might doodle while you think or sketch an image that comes to you. Make journaling fun and relaxed. No one will see what you write, and you may share with the group only what you choose of your reflections.

Keeping a journal or personal notebook as you move through *The Way of Scripture* is important for two reasons. First, the process of writing down thoughts clarifies them for us. They become more specific and concrete. Sometimes we really do not know what we think until we see our thoughts on paper; often the process of writing itself generates new creative insight. Second, this personal record captures our inward experience over time. Journaling helps us track changes in our thinking and growth of insight. Memories are notoriously fragile and fleeting in this regard. Specific feelings or creative connections we may have had two weeks ago or even three days ago, are hard to recall without a written record. Even though your journal cannot capture all that goes through your mind in a single reflection period, it will serve as a reminder. You will draw on these reminders during small-group meetings each week.

Begin by purchasing a book for this purpose. It can be as simple as a spiral-bound notebook or as fancy as a clothbound blank book. Some people prefer lined paper and some unlined. You will want, at minimum, something more permanent than a ring binder or paper pad. Upper Room Books has made available a Companions in Christ *Journal* that you may purchase if you wish.

When you begin the daily exercises, have your journal and pen or pencil at hand. You need not wait until you have finished reading and thinking an exercise through completely. Learn to stop and write as you go. Think on paper. Feel free to write anything that comes to you, even if it seems to be "off the topic." It may turn out to be more relevant or useful than you first believed. If the process seems clumsy at first, keep an open mind. Like any spiritual practice, it grows easier over time; and its value becomes more apparent.

Your weekly practice of journaling is shaped in the following way. The first day after the group meeting, you read the new chapter. Jot down your responses to the reading: "aha" moments, questions, points of disagreement, images, or any other reflections you wish to record. Over the next five days, you will do the exercises for the week, recording responses as they are invited. On the day of the group meeting, it will help to review what you have written through the week, perhaps marking portions you would like to share in the group. Bring your journal with you to meetings so that you can refer to it directly or refresh your memory about significant moments you want to paraphrase during discussion times. With time, you may find that journaling helps you to think out your own pattern of living and that you will be able to see more clearly how God is at work in your life.

Your Group Meeting

The weekly meeting is divided into four parts. First you will gather for a brief time of worship and prayer, which allows you to set aside the many concerns of the day and center on God's presence and guidance as you begin the group session.

During the second portion of the meeting, called Sharing Insights, the group leader will invite you to talk about your experiences with the chapter and daily exercises. The group leader will participate as a member and share his or her responses as well. Generally each member will briefly share thoughts and insights related to specific exercises. This sharing helps the group members learn and practice what it means to listen deeply. You are a community of persons seeking to listen to God and to one another so that you can live more faithfully as disciples of Christ. The group provides a supportive space to explore your listening, your spiritual practices, and your attempts to carry those practices into daily life.

This community does not function as a traditional support group where people are sometimes quick to offer advice or comment on one another's experiences. In *Companions* groups, members try to honor one another's experiences through prayerful attentiveness, affirmation, and respectful clarifying questions. The Sharing Insights part of the meeting is less meaningful when persons interrupt and comment on what is being said or try to "fix" what they see as a problem (called "cross talk"). Group members are invited to trust the Holy Spirit's guidance and help one another listen to that guidance.

The Sharing Insights time presents a unique opportunity to learn how God works differently in each life. Our journeys, while varied, enrich others' experiences. Other people's faith stories allow us to see anew how God's activity touches or addresses our lives in unexpected ways. The group will establish some ground rules to facilitate this sharing. Participants clearly need to agree that each person will speak only about his or her own beliefs, feelings, and responses and that all group members have permission to share only what and when they choose. Above all, participants should maintain confidentiality so that what is said in the group stays in the group. Spouses or close friends in the same group will need to agree between themselves on permissible boundaries of confidentiality so that the choice to reveal oneself does not inadvertently reveal intimacies to the group without the other's consent.

The leader participates in sharing, while listening and summarizing key insights that have surfaced. The leader closes this part of the meeting by calling attention to any patterns or themes that seem to have emerged from the group sharing. These patterns may point to a word God is offering to the group.

The third segment of the meeting, Deeper Explorations, gives group members an opportunity to explore a deeper dimension of God's grace, to practice related spiritual disciplines, or to explore implications of the week's theme for their church.

As it began, the group meeting ends with a brief time of worship, the Closing. Here members may lift to God needs and concerns arising from the meeting itself or express the spiritual learning of the week through symbol, ritual, and prayer.

Invitation to the Journey

We cannot journey far into the terrain of God's Word unaccompanied by the Incarnate Word—the risen Lord, our true and present guide in every dimension of Christian discipleship. The goal of the Christian life is to become fully whom God created us to be. Each of us is to become —in our own way—more and more like Jesus Christ, "the image of the invisible God" (Col. 1:15). It is the Holy Spirit's great work and delight to conform us to the image of Christ (2 Cor. 3:18). Therefore the weeks you give to *The Way of Scripture* offer a unique opportunity to focus on your relationship with the Holy Spirit through whom you will receive God's word as one of personal guidance, insight, and call.

We invite you now to seek the grace of the Spirit as you begin *The Way of Scripture*. Open your heart to all God desires to pour out upon you and your companions as you explore together the gift of scripture. Enter this experience with joyful anticipation of God's rich blessings. May the grace of the Holy Spirit guide your ears, eyes, and hearts as you discern and absorb the living, transforming Word.

Scripture: A Place of Transforming Encounter

A story is told about surveyors who came across a lake (now known as Lake Mohonk) in the Adirondack Mountains. They thought that measuring the depth of the lake would be a simple matter, since it was relatively small and located in what appeared to be a shallow valley between the mountains. To their surprise, when they dropped a measuring line into the lake, they didn't find the bottom. They brought in a longer line with the same results. Even the longest line available failed to find the bottom of the lake. Finally they discovered that what had appeared to be a shallow pond was a water-filled crevasse of great depth. Things aren't always what they seem.

We often make the same mistake with scripture. Like the surveyors, many of us come to scripture assuming we know quite well what we are dealing with. Through Sunday school, church, or other life influences, we developed an understanding of scripture in our minds. Whenever we open the Bible, this established understanding takes over and determines our encounter with the text. The assumptions we bring to scripture, like those of the Lake Mohonk surveyors, may distort our understanding of God's Word and its role in our spiritual journey. If we seek to probe the depths of scripture, however, like the surveyors we will discover unimagined depths that challenge many of our assumptions. We need then to probe the nature

of scripture before we can discuss methods for allowing this sacred text to play a vital role in our spiritual growth.

Here is my set of working assumptions as to the nature of scripture: (1) The Word became text (2) to provide a place of transforming encounter with God (3) so that the Word might become flesh in us (4) for the sake of the world. Let's explore each part of this proposal.

The Word Became Text

The term *scripture* has a wide range of understandings. We can simplify this diversity somewhat by considering two basic frames of reference. One frame deems scripture a divine document. The most extreme form of this view sees scripture as having been dictated by God to human writers who simply recorded what God said. A less extreme view allows human agents minor flexibility in expressing God's message. The "divine" frame of reference emphasizes scripture as an inerrant, infallible set of propositional truths. This view can make the Bible a weapon with which to coerce or manipulate persons and faith communities into the worldview, values, and lifestyle of its interpreters. Scripture then becomes a collection of inflexible rules and regulations, dos and don'ts that more often aim to maintain the community's sense of identity than to nurture a deeply spiritual life "hid with Christ in God" (Col 3:3).

The second basic frame of reference views scripture as a human document. The most extreme form of this view understands the Bible to be a completely human product, no different from any other human document. Rather than having actually influenced the writing, God becomes the subject about which humans have chosen to write. A less extreme form of this view sees scripture as recording a variety of human experiences with God. These experiences, however, tend to be human in origin and are understood within the framework of ordinary human life. This approach can result in scripture's being continually reshaped by the worldview, values, and lifestyle of those who interpret it.

Christian Scripture itself is a diverse, multi-stranded witness reflecting diverse social and historical circumstances.

—Stephen E. Fowl and L. Gregory Jones

Must we choose one of these ways of seeing scripture over the other? Much of the polarization seen in Christianity today takes root in the choice of one of these two basic options. Entire structures of theology, doctrine, liturgy, ecclesiology, and ethics are constructed upon each view, then vigorously defended against those who hold the opposing view. I would suggest an alternative.

"The Word became flesh" (John 1:14) is one of the core statements of Christian faith. As John's Gospel puts it, the Word that was in the beginning, the Word that was with God and was God, the Word through whom all things came into being, the Word that was life— this Word became human. Ever since this event, the mystery of divine-human Incarnation has puzzled the human mind. Some people have emphasized the divine aspect of the Incarnation to the exclusion of the human; some have emphasized the human aspect of the Incarnation to the exclusion of the divine; and some have held that Jesus was neither fully divine nor fully human.[1] The best attempts to resolve this mystery have revolved around an understanding that the Word made flesh was *both* fully divine and fully human.

I would propose another incarnational mystery—that the Word also became text and would further suggest an analogy between the Word-become-flesh and the Word-become-text. In the mystery of an incarnational God, Jesus is both fully God and fully human. In that same mystery, the text is both fully divine and fully human.

My proposal no doubt prompts the same kinds of questions that people raised about the Word-become-flesh. Like their views of Jesus, those who focus on the divine aspect of the Word-become-text minimize the human; those who focus on the human dimension of the Word-become-text minimize the divine. In both the Word-become-flesh and the Word-become-text, the Incarnation has experienced misunderstanding, abuse, and rejection at human hands. Those who see Jesus as merely human miss the presence of God in him. Those who see the text as merely human, miss the possibility of genuine encounter with God in its pages.

---

1. See the history of the early Gnostics, the Ebionites of the first few centuries of the Christian movement, and the Arians of the fourth century, respectively.

How then did, or does, the Word become text? Usually, we would approach this question through the concept of inspiration. The nature of inspiration, however, is as thorny as the nature of Incarnation. Was the *writer* inspired to produce the text through dictation or some other means? Was the *text* inspired by some means apart from the writer or reader? Is it the *reader* who is inspired? The Bible itself does not provide much assistance with these questions. To be sure, Peter[2] says that *no prophecy[3] of scripture is a matter of one's private interpretation because no prophecy was ever motivated[4] by human will, but persons being motivated by the Holy Spirit spoke from God* (2 Pet. 1:20-21).[5] Peter deals with the three essential dimensions of any text: the writer ("people motivated by the Holy Spirit spoke from God"), the text itself ("prophecy"), and the reader ("a matter of one's private interpretation"). What is Peter trying to convey?

First, Peter makes it clear that God addresses persons, God encounters *us*. The initiative comes from God's side, not ours. Second, God addresses or encounters us through a text that has come into existence through persons speaking out of their experience of the Holy Spirit's motivation. In other words, the text emerges from the deeply intimate and experiential relationship the writers had with God. Peter's phrasing in the Greek is significant: *persons* while being motivated *by the Holy Spirit spoke from God*. Their speaking comes out of their experience with God. Third, readers may not simply freely interpret the text from their personal frame of reference. The text is not a foundation on which readers can build a structure of meaning to suit or confirm their own worldview, values, and lifestyle.

Peter seems to indicate that the reading of scripture falls under the same guidelines as its writing. When the reader is "motivated by the Holy Spirit," the text becomes a place of deep, intimate, experiential

2. In referencing New Testament books where authorship is questioned by scholars, traditional attributions of authorship will be used.

3 "Prophecy" in scripture is not primarily a matter of foretelling the future but rather of speaking for God into the contemporary human context of the speaker and hearers.

4. The Greek term translated here as *motivated* means "to carry, bear, produce, bring forth, engender."

5. All translations are M. Robert Mulholland Jr.'s unless otherwise noted.

relationship with God. Just as the writer spoke from God under the movement of the Spirit, so the reader hears God speak through the text while being moved by the same Spirit.

In the only other biblical passage that touches on the inspiration of the text, Paul seems to wrestle with the same reality. He speaks of "every God-breathed writing" (2 Tim. 3:16), using a term (*God-breathed*) that appears only here in the whole Bible. In the oral culture of Paul's day, written texts always implied a hearer as well as a speaker. We might infer from this that the "God-breathed" nature of the address was as essential for the hearer as the speaker or for the reader as the writer. Paul may be indicating that the writing is "God-breathed" in its reception as well as in its inception.

Seemingly, then, the "how" of the Word's becoming text is a dynamic process that involves both writer and reader. John Wesley reflects this understanding when he writes, "Scripture can only be understood through the same Spirit whereby it was given."[6] Inspiration is a dynamic interplay of the Spirit with both the writer and the reader. From the writers' side, inspiration is an established reality. From the readers' side, it is a potential reality. When, as readers, we open ourselves to God's presence, we complete the circuit; the Word becomes text—a place full of possibilities for divine encounter.

To Provide a Place of Transforming Encounter with God

Renowned Trappist monk Thomas Merton wrote:

> It is of the very nature of the Bible to affront, perplex, and astonish the human mind. Hence the reader who opens the Bible must be prepared for disorientation, confusion, incomprehension, perhaps outrage.[7]

I doubt this list of feelings comes to mind in our reading of the Bible. Merton implies that the Bible is not a comfortable collection of stories, sayings, teachings, and history from which we may glean

---

6. John Wesley, *The Works of John Wesley*, 3rd ed. (Kansas City, MO: Beacon Hill Press, 1872), 14:253.

7. Thomas Merton, *Opening the Bible* (Collegeville, MN: Liturgical Press, 1970), 1.

information to enhance our knowledge or buttress our worldview. Merton uses the language of encounter, confrontation, and transformation. The Bible, as the Word-become-text, often confronts our well-established ideas. It can astonish us with a radically different value system that challenges our conformity to prevailing cultural values. When this occurs, we find ourselves disoriented and confused. It feels as if our world is being turned upside down. What we encounter may seem incomprehensible from the perspective of our established way of life, and we may be outraged that anyone would have the nerve to question our way of being in the world.

Our problem lies in assuming that life should be understood from within the framework of *our* worldview. We judge and value almost everything in our life on the basis of this assumption. To be sure, if we have a little maturity, we admit to some rough edges in our way of life that need to be smoothed out or a few gaps that need to be filled—but always within the larger frame of our basic worldview. Rarely do we entertain the possibility that our entire understanding of life may require profound transformation.

Such transformation, however, is the primary purpose of the Word-become-text. Listen again to Merton: "The basic claim made by the Bible for the word of God is not so much that it is to be blindly accepted because of God's authority, but that *it is recognized by its transforming and liberating power.*"[8] And again, "Involvement is dangerous, because it lays one open to unforeseen conclusions."[9] To come to scripture without true desire for a transforming encounter with God is to bring the text under our control and make it a means of self-improvement at best and a confirmation of our present way of life at worst. In either case we do no serious grappling with our need for deep transformation, our need to lose our entire self-focused way of being so that we might become God-focused beings.

Paul sums up the transformative nature of the Word-become-text this way:

Bonhoeffer . . . discovered the importance of allowing Scripture to challenge the presumptions with which we come to the text.

—Stephen E. Fowl and
L. Gregory Jones

8. Ibid., 8.
9. Ibid., 33.

All God-breathed writing is valuable for teaching, for refutation of error, for correction of deficiencies, for nurture in loving union with God,[10] in order that God-referenced persons might be all they were created to be,[11] having been designed[12] for every good work (2 Tim. 3:16-17).

Let's walk through this passage.

The Word-become-text is valuable for teaching. I hope by now you see that this does *not* mean the Bible is merely a textbook of information for the reader to absorb. Although scripture presents us with a wealth of information, the goal of this information is transformation not education. When the word *teaching* appears in plural form in the New Testament, it refers either to human teachings or the teaching of demons.[13] When the word appears in the singular form, as it does here, it refers to the nature of a God-centered way of life and God's reign that finds expression in such a life.[14] The Word-become-text encounters us with the reality of God's realm of being and its hallmark of the God-focused way of life.

The Word-become-text is also valuable for refutation of error. This flows naturally and inseparably from the *teaching.* When we encounter God's realm of being and its worldview, values, and lifestyle that are so contrary to those of our world, our involvement in the false and dehumanizing values of the world are revealed in the light of Reality. We are confronted with the destructive path on which we are walking and, if we have eyes to see, convinced of the futility of that path. The Word-become-text challenges our deadness with Life, our darkness with Light, our brokenness with Wholeness, our woundedness with Healing, our bondage with Liberation.

---

10. The Greek for the usual translation, "righteousness," is Paul's term for right relationship with God. This is not merely a legally right relationship, that is, that God has ruled in our favor against the alienation caused by our willful separation, but rather the restoration of that relationship of loving union with God for which we were created.

11. The Greek term usually translated "complete" describes something that is the epitome of what it was intended to be.

12. The Greek word usually rendered "equipped" is a compound verb indicating that becoming all we were created to be is not our doing but God's transforming work in us.

13. See, for example, Colossians 2:22 and 1 Timothy 4:1.

14. See, for example, 1 Timothy 4:6, 13, 16; 2 Timothy 3:10; Titus 2:1, 7.

The Word-become-text is valuable for correction of deficiencies. This aspect works in tandem with refuting error. As we have seen, the Word-become-text refutes the error of our lives by revealing what God intends us to be. Instead of beating us into the ground with our faults and failures, it holds before us an alternative way of being. Seeing in sharp clarity the deficiency of what we have been is more than compensated by the compelling vision of what we are to become as persons created in God's image.

Such a vision, however, can overwhelm us. Having fallen so far from what we were created to be, we resemble couch potatoes being called to become world-class athletes! Poor habits and attitudes, entrenched by years of practice, can incapacitate us. We are broken by circumstances and wounded by relationships. Painful memories often become reservoirs of guilt, resentment, and bitterness, poisoning the well of our relationships with others and infecting our whole way of engaging life.

In our depths of despair, *the Word-become-text offers us nurture into loving union with God.* The word *nurture* indicates a process. The Greek term[15] described the process by which an infant was trained, educated, disciplined, socialized, and matured into full adulthood in the worldview, value system, and lifestyle of the community. An infant does not become a mature adult instantly; a couch potato does not become a world-class athlete in a week, and we do not become persons deeply conformed to the image of Christ in three simple steps. The Word-become-text becomes our "trainer." As we yield ourselves to the trainer's disciplines, our self-focused worldview gradually gives way to a more God-focused worldview. As we meet daily with the trainer, our self-serving value system undergoes a profound shift to a God- and other-serving value system. As we incarnate the trainer's truths, our self-pleasing lifestyle slowly shifts into a Christlike way of living in the world.

Through the transformation process we grow ever deeper into the loving union with God for which we were created and into which

> *But the call is to read Scripture over-against ourselves, allowing Scripture to question our lives.*
>
> —Stephen E. Fowl and L. Gregory Jones

---

15. *Paideia* from which we get our word *pedagogy*.

God continually nurtures us. In this relationship we respond to God's total self-giving to us in love with the free abandonment of ourselves to God in utter God-centered love.

The Word-become-text nurtures us into loving union with God; through this transforming encounter we become what God intends us to be, persons in God's own image. Our transformation into Christlikeness draws us into God's design, and we become persons through whom God's love, mercy, and grace touches others.

That the Word Might Become Flesh in Us

Does this seem like an exaggerated or even outrageous claim? Certainly the Word became flesh in Jesus, but in *us*? Yet several intriguing passages in the New Testament point in this direction. For example, in one of his descriptions of Jesus, Paul says, "In him all the fullness of God was pleased to dwell" (Col. 1:19). This does not surprise us. It fits well with Paul's teaching that "God was in Christ" (2 Cor. 5:19). Jesus himself said, "I and the Father are one" (John 10:30) and "The one who has seen me has seen the Father" (John 14:9). But then Paul prays for the Ephesians (and us) "that you may be filled with all the fullness of God" (Eph. 3:19). Does Paul really expect believers to be like Jesus to this extent? Perhaps such an idea has never occurred to us nor been encouraged in our Christian upbringing.

Yet Paul is not alone in his claim. Peter makes a similar assertion when he writes the following:

> God's divine power has given to us all the things we need for life, a godly life, through the relationship[16] we have with the one who called us to his own likeness[17] and goodness, through which God has given us priceless and magnificent promises so that through these we might become partakers of the divine nature having escaped the destructiveness of the world's desires (2 Pet. 1:3-4).

16. Most translations have "through the knowledge of the one who called us." The Greek term for "knowledge" is more often used for experiential knowledge than cognitive knowledge. Thus, what is given is not information but a relationship.

17. The term *glory* (*doxa*), which I have translated as "likeness," will be discussed shortly.

"Partakers of the divine nature" seems to be Peter's equivalent of Paul's "being filled with all the fullness of God." Where do Peter and Paul get this idea?

It seems they got it from Jesus.[18] Chapter 17 of John's Gospel records Jesus' "high priestly prayer." After praying for the eleven disciples who remain with him (vv. 1-19), Jesus prays "for those believing in me through their word" (v. 20). This is Jesus' prayer for all believers of all times. He prays "that they may all be one" (v. 21*a*). What does he mean by *one*? Is Jesus praying for theological unity? doctrinal unity? ecclesiological unity? liturgical unity? Reviewing the history of the church through two millennia, it would appear that on none of these counts has Jesus' prayer ever been fulfilled. If we look more closely, however, we see what Jesus meant by one. His prayer continues, "that they may all be one in exactly the same way[19] you, Father, are in me and I am in you" (17:21). Jesus is praying that believers will be in exactly the same relationship of loving union with God that he is. He even continues, "in order that they might be in us" (17:21), implying something of a trinitarian joining of God, Jesus, and believers in a relationship of loving union.

We could interpret this passage in other ways, but we receive confirmation of this understanding in the next statement of Jesus' prayer: "The glory you have given me I have given to them, in order that they might be one in exactly the same way we are one" (17:22). What is this glory? The Greek word translated "glory" signifies those essential aspects of persons or things that make them what they are. God's glory is the very nature of divine being—the essence of who God is. The glory God gave Jesus is God's very nature: "The Word became flesh and dwelt among us, and we have seen his glory, the unique glory of the Father" (John 1:14).

18. It is unlikely that either Peter or Paul had John's Gospel available to them. Peter would have learned from Jesus himself what John included in his Gospel. While Paul may have learned this from Peter or other apostles, it is likely that he came to this understanding through his deep, intimate life in Christ.

19. The Greek term here is a compounded adverb which means "just as," "in exactly the same manner," "to the degree that." Later in John, Jesus says to the disciples, "In exactly the same way the Father sent me, I send you" (20:21).

We may find it difficult to accept that Jesus has given this glory to us! Just as the Word became flesh in him, the Word is also to become flesh in us. It may help us grasp this astonishing reality to look further at Paul's use of the word *glory* in his letters.

All have sinned and become less than the glory of God (Rom. 3:23). God created us for participation in divine glory, but we have become less than what we were meant to be. Two chapters later Paul says, "We rejoice in our hope of the glory of God" (Rom. 5:2), indicating possible restoration. In Colossians, Paul reveals the mystery of the Gospel: "Christ in you the hope of glory" (1:27); the indwelling presence of Christ restores us to our true nature in the image and likeness of God. Again Paul says, "We all with unveiled faces beholding the glory of the Lord are being transformed into the same likeness, from glory into glory" (2 Cor. 3:18)—from what we are in our unlikeness to God to the likeness of the divine image. It seems clear that the glory of Christ has restored us in the image of God. Our loving union with God serves as the central expression of our restored glory, and we fulfill Jesus' prayer that we might be one in exactly the same way they are one.

Perhaps an illustration will help. Imagine the score of a Beethoven symphony (or another composer if Beethoven is not your favorite). The score corresponds to a text that has vocabulary (notes), grammar (notes play different roles depending upon their form and location on the clef), syntax (the harmonies, rhythms, and dynamics of the piece), sociological context (the different families of instruments), and content (the various themes developed in the piece). Beethoven heard the symphony in his being and wrote the score from his intimate relationship with the music that resonated within him. In other words, the symphony became "text." We could analyze the score as a text, gather information from it, even develop a perfect musicological understanding of it. But that is not the text's primary purpose. Beethoven wrote the score so that the music-become-text might become flesh in the rich sound of a symphony orchestra.

The biblical writers heard the music of God's transformative symphony in their intimate relationship with God; out of their experience with this music, they created the "score" of that symphony. The Word

> *The glory of God is the human being fully alive.*
>
> —Irenaeus of Lyons

25

whose harmonies and rhythms resonated deeply in their beings became text through their hands so others might experience the transforming music of the Word and play it forth in their lives. The Word became text to provide a place of transforming encounter with God, so that the Word might become flesh again in us. Yet this incarnation is not merely a private, personal solitude with God.

For the Sake of the World

In his prayer, Jesus cites a specific purpose for the relationship of loving union with God. He notes a vital intention for being restored in the glory of God: "that the world might believe that you sent me" (17:21) and "that the world might know that you sent me" (17:23). The world will not believe and know that God sent Jesus because our theology is true, our doctrine correct, and our liturgy proper. The world will know and believe *when it sees Jesus in us.*

The Word becomes flesh *in* us so that God's transforming love might touch a broken and hurting world *through* us. We are to be those in whom God's life touches people enmeshed in the deadly illusions of the world; those in whom God's light illumines the darkness of persons blinded by the world's false values; those through whom God's healing touches the wounds of people crippled by the corrosive lifestyle of the world; those in whom God's wholeness touches persons broken in body, mind, or spirit by the pernicious perspectives of the world; those through whom God's cleansing touches people stained by sin; those through whom God's liberating grace frees people held in the bondage of dehumanizing attitudes, habits, and addictions; those through whom God's transforming love challenges social, cultural, political, and economic systems that disfigure human communities.

We will not find the ultimate meaning of scripture in an intellectual construct or formula. The meaning of scripture is incarnational. We never *know* scripture until we have allowed it to be a means of God's transforming grace, empowering us to live the reality of the Word into our world. Thus, we cannot know or understand "love

We do not practice lectio divina *for the purpose of textual study, . . . but to know and to love God.*

—García M. Colombás

your enemies" through discussion or careful definitions of *enemy* and *love*. Love of enemies can only be known by abandoning ourselves to God in loving union, being radically available to God for the enemy so that we become the means of God's presence and grace in the enemy's life.

The Way of Scripture is not simply another Bible study, not simply another spiritual practice to enhance our personal piety or insure our welcome in heaven. *The Way of Scripture* aims to bring us into a continually transforming encounter with God, so that the Word might become flesh in us for the sake of the world God loves so much.

DAILY EXERCISES

Before beginning these exercises read, Week 1, "Scripture: A Place of Transforming Encounter." Make notes in your journal as you read the chapter, recording your insights and questions. Then use your journal regularly as you engage in these exercises. Focusing on one exercise each day will help you build a daily pattern of reflection and prayer in your life. Give yourself the gift of a quiet space apart for this time of prayer, opening your mind and heart to the leading of God's Spirit.

EXERCISE 1

Reread the opening story of the Lake Mohonk surveyors (page 15). Reflect on your own experience of reading and hearing the Bible read. Where have you known surprise, incomprehension, or deep questioning in your encounter with this book? What scripture passages most challenge your assumptions about God's nature? What parts of the Bible make you wonder why we call this book God's Word?

Draw a picture of the Lake Mohonk crevasse—perhaps a deep V-shape below a waterline. At the water's surface and near the top of the lake, list a few Bible stories or teachings that seem clear to you in their meaning. Farther down the crevasse, name some passages or stories that don't fit with your understanding of life or faith. Near the bottom of the fissure, list passages that seem a total mystery to you. Offer these to God in prayer with hope and trust that your understanding will grow, even if you may never fully comprehend. Give thanks for God's mystery and rest in a sense of "unknowing" trust.

EXERCISE 2

Read 2 Peter 1:20-21. How do these verses speak to your heart about the nature of scripture? Reread the author's paragraphs about this text (see pages 18–19). How do you understand the relationship among the biblical writers, the Spirit of God, the text, and you as reader? Put words to this understanding in your journal, even if it feels tentative or awkward to you.

Give thanks for the role of the Holy Spirit in the writing of scripture and the work of interpreting God's Word in your heart. Pray for openness to new understandings and experiences in the coming weeks as you join with others to explore the Bible more deeply. Pray that each person in your Companions group be open to new learning and growth, so that your time together may express and glorify God's reign.

EXERCISE 3

Read Isaiah 55:8-9. Recall from memory a biblical situation that reflected a radically different value system from our current cultural values. Make notes in your journal.

Look closely at Jesus' teachings in Luke 6:20-36. What in your life needs to be transformed by the values of God's Word expressed here? Let each phrase or idea of Jesus' teaching guide you into a personal prayer of confession. Write your prayer in your journal. When you finish, receive God's assurance of forgiveness and seek divine strength for commitment to live your life out of Christ's values.

EXERCISE 4

Read several of the texts used in the section of this chapter titled "That the Word Might Become Flesh in Us": Ephesians 3:19; 2 Peter 1:3-4; John 17:20-22; 2 Corinthians 3:18. Which verses especially strike you? What do you find easy to accept, and what is difficult to believe?

Write a letter to God expressing your feelings, marvelings, questions. Listen for how you sense God may be responding to your letter. Rest in gratitude.

EXERCISE 5

Read James 1:22-27; 2:18. What in these passages speaks to you? Spend some time considering the image of looking "in a mirror" and then forgetting what you see. How have you experienced "seeing" and then "forgetting" in your life? When has a scripture passage shown you something about yourself you hadn't recognized before? How did this recognition change your way of being in the world? Respond to these questions in your journal.

From these reflections, set an intention for this day or the next. Where do you hear God calling you to a new way to live the message you are receiving? Write a word or two that captures your intention, and place it where you will see it several times daily (bathroom mirror, computer screen, car dashboard). Or you might prefer to find a small object that represents your intention and carry it in your pocket or purse.

Review the week's journal entries in preparation for the group meeting.

Silentio: Preparing to Be Read by Scripture

The Word became text to provide a place of transforming encounter with God so that the Word might become flesh in us in our world. How, then, do we approach the text so as to experience this transforming encounter? Many Christians give little or no regular attention to scripture. For some who do, it is merely a pious exercise to check off the list of daily spiritual practices. For others it reflects a duty to prepare for a Sunday school lesson, a sermon, or some special responsibility. Thomas Merton states it well:

> Curiously, the most serious religious people, or the most concerned scholars, those who constantly read the Bible as a matter of professional or pious duty, can often manage to evade a radically involved dialogue with the book. . . .
>
> Those for whom the Bible has become a habit may well defraud themselves of deeper understanding by deciding in advance what they want of the Bible and what it wants of them.[1]

Simply put, the motive and manner of our approach to scripture determine in large measure our experience with it.

What thoughts and images come to your mind when you hear the word *Bible* or *scripture*? How well integrated into your daily life are these ideas and pictures? Where do they reside in your awareness—

---

1. Merton, *Opening the Bible*, 24, 26.

*Scripture does not
constitute one
instrument among
others that help one to
progress in the life of
the spirit. . . .
The spiritual life . . .
consists of the reading
of the Bible,
meditated, understood
and lived.*

—García M. Colombás

on the edge, detached from the realities of daily existence, reserved for the "religious" dimension of your life?

If we take our companionship with Christ seriously—intent on deepening a relationship of loving union with God in Christ, focused on allowing the Word to become flesh in us in our corner of the world—then scripture will be as essential to us as breathing. However, making the Bible a core essential of our life and allowing it to be a place of transforming encounter with God are different matters. We can make scripture a core essential in our life yet not experience it as a place of transforming encounter with God. Then it is central only as a pious duty or professional responsibility. But we will not experience scripture as a place of transforming encounter unless it is a core essential. We must first decide whether to let scripture become a central feature of our life. We often carefully nurture our bodies for the sake of good health and effective work. How much more intentional we need to be about nurturing our life with God!

Suppose we have recognized scripture as a vital means of grace through which God draws us ever deeper into loving union, transforming us into Christlikeness. How do we approach the Word-become-text so that it consistently becomes a place of transforming encounter? What knowledge do we need to acquire? What techniques do we need to learn, or what methods do we need to practice? Beginning with knowledge, techniques, and methods misses the mark. Our functionally oriented culture suggests that our first response to any need is to "do" something. Listen to strangers who meet for the first time. Within a minute of conversation, one will inevitably ask the other, "What do you do?" Occupation or job title is one of our culture's primary means of identity. We tend to label, classify, and value people on the basis of what they do. We also find some of the deepest roots of our own identity in what we do. Naturally, we are inclined to value others and ourselves based on how well we do what we do. No wonder our initial response to a problem or need is, "What do I need to do?" So when we realize that scripture is meant to be a place of transforming encounter with God, our primary reaction is, "What do I do to experience this transformation?"

Yet we are not first of all human *doings* but human *beings.* Someone has wisely turned the old quip around so it goes, "Don't just do something, stand there!" This acknowledges being rather than doing as primary. Our functional culture thinks that being derives from doing when, in truth, doing is the expression of being. If our being depends on doing, then we are the creators of our own being. And the "being" that results is anxious, harried, and troubled—always feeling that something vital is missing, ever striving to do more in hopes of becoming less anxious, harried, and troubled!

Have you ever noticed that Jesus' first temptation is to make his being dependent on his doing? Jesus' temptations follow his baptism at which the heavenly voice affirms, "You are my son, the beloved, in you I have taken delight" (Mark 1:11; Luke 3:22).[2] In these words we hear the divine identification of Jesus' being. After Jesus has fasted forty days, the tempter first questions his being—"*If* you are the son of God," then slyly suggests that *who Jesus is* is grounded in *what he does*—"speak to this stone in order that it might become bread" (Luke 4:3). This action implies that Jesus' ability to turn stones into bread proves his identity as God's Son. While this may not be the only interpretation of the text, Jesus' response reveals it to be a valid interpretation: "It is written, humanity will not live by bread alone, but by every word coming forth through the mouth of God" (Matt. 4:4).[3] In other words, human *being* is not derived from *doing* (bread alone) but is spoken forth by God. The text also suggests that God continually speaks us forth into being.[4]

At the beginning of this chapter I proposed that "the motive and manner" of our approach to scripture largely determine our experience with it. While motive and manner *can* express our doing, in this case I intend that they express our being. We need to reorient our inner being as we engage scripture; in particular, to abandon our

> *The Bible raises the question of identity in a way no other book does.*
>
> —Thomas Merton

---

2. The words in Mark and Luke are identical. Matthew differs slightly: "This is my son, the beloved, in whom I have taken delight" (3:17). All three focus on Jesus' identity as God's son.

3. Luke abbreviates the response: "It is written, humanity will not live by bread alone" (Luke 4:4).

4. The Greek grammar (present participle) indicates continuous action in relation to the primary verb "will live." For fuller development of this idea, see my book *Shaped by the Word: The Power of Scripture in Spiritual Formation* (Nashville, TN: Upper Room Books, 2000), 34.

functional orientation. I call this reorientation *silentio* (Latin for "silence"). We will consider *silentio* in its proper context.

Our Christian heritage contains a rich traditional practice known as *lectio divina*, meaning "spiritual reading" and often referred to simply as *lectio*.[5] The roots of *lectio* are hidden in the mists of early Christian history. We find one of the earliest formulations of the practice in *The Rule of Saint Benedict* from the sixth century. Benedict, however, received this discipline from his predecessors. Most likely it emerged from the spiritual practices of the desert fathers and mothers of the first centuries of the Christian movement. Throughout Christian history, *lectio* has been close to the heart of the great spiritual mothers and fathers. They realized that only by drinking in the Word and being steeped in it could their lives be shaped by the Word into Christlikeness for the sake of the world. The classical discipline of *lectio divina* intertwines four movements: *lectio, meditatio, oratio,* and *contemplatio.* We will explore each of these four phases in later chapters. I have taken the liberty of adding a preliminary step (*silentio*) and a final movement (*incarnatio*) as an aid to the modern practice of this ancient prayer path.

Before delving into the practice of *lectio divina*, it is important to reflect on the inner orientation we bring to the act of reading; that is, to the nature of our being as we come into the presence of the Word-become-text. Through most of Christian history, monastic communities provided the context for the practice of *lectio*. Those practicing the discipline inhabited an environment in which they sought to deepen their relationship with God. They dwelt, spirit and soul, in the divine presence that pervaded their entire world. We no longer live in such a world.

We tend to think of ourselves as individuals whose being is totally distinct from what is outside of us. So we view virtually everything from a self-focused perspective. Circumstances and relationships all revolve around our personal experiences, feelings, and ideas. This

We force the Bible to conform to our own views rather than allowing the Bible to form us into God's people.

—Daniel Wolpert

---

5. *Lectio* is pronounced lex-ee-oh. For a more complete description of the classic stages of *lectio divina*, see "A Basic Pattern of Meditation" and "Helpful Guidelines" of the *Companions in Christ* Participant's Book (pages 86–91).

subtle but deeply entrenched orientation suffuses the views, values, and behaviors that shape our way of being in the world. As a result, the Bible becomes one more thing in orbit around our self-focused being. We determine the importance of its orbit to us, the implications of its presence for our way of being. We determine the role of scripture in our life. Our valuing of scripture is the "gravity" that controls whether its orbit is close or distant to our heart.

For scripture to become a place of truly transforming encounter with God, we need a complete reorientation: the Word becomes the central focal point—with us in orbit around it! Or, to change the metaphor, we let the text become the "subject" and ourselves become the "object" of the text's attention. Typically we see ourselves as the subject and the text as the object of *our* attention. We come to the Bible for what we want; we read into it our own worldview; we find in it a reflection of our value system; we discover in it the confirmation of our lifestyle. The Bible will confront us only if we allow the text to challenge our way of being.

For those of us who need a fundamental reorientation of our approach to scripture, *silentio* describes one approach to this reordering. For scripture to become a place of transforming encounter with God, our old ways of approaching it need to be silenced. Unless you have never read the Bible before, you probably bring an entrenched posture or attitude to the text. Even if you are coming to scripture for the first time, you likely have some preconceptions about what the Bible is, how you should read it, and what it should mean. Those of us for whom Bible reading is a devotional or professional duty have certainly developed habits of perception and procedure that come into play when we open scripture.

Generally, the entrenched positions we bring to scripture help us maintain control over the text. We want to keep the text at a safe distance, to establish the limits of its place in our life. We don't want the Word to confront deep-rooted injustices in our worldview; to challenge our self-focused value system; to raise troubling questions about our worldly lifestyle. Basically, we want scripture to endorse our way of being in the world, affirm our value system, and confirm our

When we go to sit in silence, when we turn our minds to our Creator, we begin the process of allowing God to be the center of our world.

—Daniel Wolpert

lifestyle. This is precisely what happens when we imprison the Bible in the narrow walls of the entrenched positions we bring to the text.

A related danger involves the assumption that our way of reading scripture is normative; our interpretation of the Bible is correct and therefore should be imposed upon others. When this happens, scripture is no longer the Word-become-text to provide a place of transforming encounter with God; it becomes the captive of our views and values, providing justification for the injustices we perpetrate upon others. At worst it becomes a means of bringing others under our control.

For scripture to become a place of transforming encounter with God requires a radical reorientation of being. *Silentio* is the discipline of stilling the noise of entrenched positions we bring to the text.

The first step in *silentio* comes in acknowledging the noise. When we try to become still in our being, we discover the cacophony within: we recall duties and responsibilities that weigh on us, competing for our time and attention; we find needs and desires that demand consideration; we discover deep wounds from our past that spew bitterness and resentment into our spirit; we discover relationships of dependency or bondage that distort our life. Any one of these distractions can monopolize our attention, or they can compete for our attention by pulling us out of centeredness to bounce haphazardly among their voices. We need to learn to acknowledge this noise within and then set it aside as we focus on God. Sometimes a simple phrase, repeated slowly and steadily, helps us silence the noise: "Hid with Christ in God" (Col. 3:3), or "You are the center of my being," or "You alone, . . . you alone, . . . you alone." If we make value judgments on the "noise," our judgments become a further distraction. True valuing will emerge out of centeredness in God. *Silentio* can allow scripture to become a place of transforming encounter with God.

Of course, the idea of transformation may be disturbing or troubling. The entire universe of internal noise that demands our attention and shapes our identity also serves to protect us against the rigors of real transformation. Genuine change can feel so threatening that we take refuge in mental distractions as a defense. But when we

The most formidable enemy of the spiritual life . . . is self-deception; and if there is a better cure for self-deception than silence, it has yet to be discovered.

—E. Herman

willingly face the Spirit's transforming work and center ourselves in God, the noise in our heads begins to change. Our perceptions may undergo genuine restructuring that shifts what we thought was vital to relative unimportance and turns what we believed to be minor into a major part of our life with God. Our value system may get shaken up, our understanding of right and wrong turned on its head. This restructure may seriously challenge our comfortable lifestyle and radically reorder our priorities.

The second step in *silentio* requires our letting go of an entrenched approach to scripture. Indeed, we might call *silentio* the practice of abandonment. As noted earlier, we do not come to the Bible totally free of preconceptions, formed either through our own history with scripture or the way others have imprinted ideas about it on our minds. In either case, we tend to perceive scripture as an object out-side ourselves that we can either disregard or use for our own purposes. We perceive scripture as a resource we can tap whenever we think it might provide something we want or need. This turns the Bible into a mere "tool" whose use is determined by our agenda.

If, however, scripture is the Word-become-text, it is not merely an object for our use according to our whims. It is, in a real sense, the pres-ence of God. Imagine how you would enter a room if you knew God awaited you and desired to speak with you. I suspect you would not casually stroll into the room to see whether or not God had anything interesting to say. I doubt you would receive whatever God said to you as advice you could take or ignore as you wished, as if the divine Word was merely one option among others you could select at will. Why, then, would we treat the Word-become-text any differently?

Silentio, the discipline of coming to scripture as we would come to God, may require a serious reorientation of our view of the Bible and our posture toward it. We will need to come to grips with our entrenched approach to scripture and wrestle with how to release it.

In the third step of *silentio*, we come to scripture with a deep inner posture of stillness, listening, receptivity, and a readiness to respond to the least whisper of the Word. John Wesley advises us "to read . . . with a single eye, to know the whole will of God, . . . [with]

Words can be ways of hiding from the Word, rather than means of allowing ourselves to be formed by it.

—Norvene Vest

a fixed resolution to do it."[6] Both parts of this advice are crucial dimensions of *silentio*. It is one thing to want to *know* the whole will of God, quite another to have a "fixed resolution to do it." The book of Exodus offers a good illustration of this truth. Israel has finally arrived at Sinai (19:2) after a wandering, three-month escape from Egypt (13:18–19:2). God calls Moses up to Mount Sinai and says to him, "Thus you shall say to the house of Jacob, and tell the Israelites: . . . if you obey my voice and keep my covenant, you shall be my treasured possession out of all the peoples. . . . You shall be for me a priestly kingdom and a holy nation" (19:3-5, NRSV). Moses gathers the elders of the tribes and gives them this message (19:7). Presumably the elders canvass their tribes, for the next thing we hear is Israel's response, "Everything that the LORD has spoken we will do" (19:8, NRSV). The intriguing part is that at this point God has not yet given a single commandment. The Ten Commandments are given in 20:1-17. God is calling the Israelites to unconditional commitment (in Wesley's words, a "fixed resolution") to do the whole will of God even before they have any idea of what it might entail.

Silentio is the discipline of coming to the Word-become-text in a deeply yielded inner posture, yearning to hear what God will say, determined to fulfill in our lives what we discern as God's message for us.

---

6. Wesley, *Works of Wesley*, 3rd ed., 14:253.

DAILY EXERCISES

Before starting these reflection exercises, read Week 2, "*Silentio*: Preparing to Be Read by Scripture." Record insights and questions in your journal. Continue making journal entries as you reflect on these exercises, one each day. It helps to have a particular time and place for this daily practice of prayerful reflection. Give yourself the gift of silence in a focused way this week, opening to God's grace and guidance.

EXERCISE 1

Spend some time reflecting on the questions (pages 31–32) at the start of the chapter: What thoughts and pictures come to your mind when you hear the word *Bible* or *scripture*? How well integrated are these ideas and images into your daily life? Write or draw what comes to mind. (You might look back at the reflection sheet on your "Personal History with the Bible" from last week's meeting.)

Reflect on the extent to which you integrate scripture into your daily life. How does scripture affect your worldview, values, and activities? In what ways does scripture simply play on the edges of your spiritual life? Record your observations.

On a scale of 1 to 10 (10 being irreplaceably essential and 1 being utterly useless) where would you put the Bible? Be totally candid with yourself. Allow your responses to lead you into a time of prayer. Capture the essence of your prayer in your journal.

EXERCISE 2

Read Luke 10:38-42. This familiar story may make us mad or glad. Ponder the story in light of the distinction made by the author between doing and being.

The chapter points out that when we believe our being depends on our doing, our being gets anxious and harried. How would you interpret Martha's approach based on this passage? How does this story speak to you of the relationship between your own doing and being? Note thoughts in your journal.

Imagine yourself as each sister. Take at least five minutes to record an imagined dialogue between the two of you. Then bring Jesus into your conversation. What is Jesus' invitation to you as Martha? What affirmation or invitation do you receive from him as Mary? What is God's primary invitation to you in this story?

EXERCISE 3

Read 1 Kings 19:11-12. Elijah has fled from Queen Jezebel's death threat, retreating to a cave on Mount Horeb. After the great wind, earthquake, and fire comes "a still small voice" or "a sound of sheer silence" (NRSV). The Lord is in the silence.

Identify some of the "noise" of your life—the winds, earthquakes, and fires. Sketch a symbolic picture in your journal for a few of these experiences, and label what they represent in your life. How much of this noise is external, how much internal?

Now reflect on a time in your life when you experienced real silence. Where were you? How did you feel? Would the "sound of sheer silence" terrify or delight you? Ponder how your life experiences have shaped your response to silence.

Allow yourself to sit in silent stillness for several minutes, listening for whatever word God may choose to offer. Let yourself relax into the gift of quiet, and don't worry if you don't hear anything. Be with God in peace.

EXERCISE 4

Read Job 2:11-13. Imagine these three friends sitting with Job for seven days and nights without speaking a word. Reflect for a few moments on where people sit together in silence in our world today, and why.

Later, these three friends will express their views of God in relation to human suffering. The Lord will refute their interpretations! How have you experienced people using the Bible to justify their own ideas? When have you done the same thing? What conventional or entrenched positions might lie behind using scripture to support a personal prejudice or ideology? Reflect in your journal.

In lectio we let a new and powerful word be born in the soil of silence.

—Norvene Vest

Being a counselor I wouldn't do it this way

40

Try to identify an assumption you bring to scripture that might be limiting. How might you silence your presupposition and invite God to reveal the meaning of scripture in the Spirit's own way and time? Pray for such grace.

EXERCISE 5

Read John 15:1-5. The same Greek root refers both to pruning and to cleansing. Ponder the possible connection between these two words and their meanings. What form might God's pruning or cleansing take in your life just now? Sketch an image.

In your imagination, become the branch abiding in the vine. How does it feel to "abide" or dwell in the life-giving force and strength of a deeply rooted vine? Do you experience abiding as more of a being or doing experience? Journal with your thoughts.

Ponder once more what needs to be pruned or cleansed in you in order to abide daily in Christ. In prayer, seek to be available to the sap of divine grace. Rest in the vine of Christ, absorbing whatever inner nutrients you need to be fruitful. You might wish to hum a song of adoration.

Review the week's journal entries in preparation for the group meeting.

Week 3
Lectio: Ingesting the Word

W hen we have silenced the inner noise of our life enough to nurture a receptive, listening posture toward God, we are ready for the first classic stage of *lectio divina*: *lectio*. *Lectio* simply means "reading." The title of this chapter, however, suggests a different kind of reading than what we are accustomed to.[1]

The moment you opened this book to read, a powerful set of pre-conditioned perceptions went into effect. You are the victim of a life-long, educationally shaped learning mode that establishes you as the controlling power (reader) who seeks to master a body of information (text) that can be used by you (technique/method) to advance your own purposes (information or, in this case, spiritual formation).

In our deeply ingrained way of reading, we are the masters. Consciously or unconsciously, we come to a text with this agenda firmly in place. If what we read does not adapt itself quickly to our sense of mastery, we usually lay it aside and look for something that does. If it adapts, we exercise control over the text by grasping it with our mind. Our rational intellect goes into full swing to analyze, critique, synthesize, and digest any material we find suited to our agenda. The text is an object outside of us that we control. We control our approach

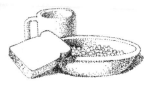

---

1. The first half of this chapter is adapted from my book *Shaped by the Word: The Power of Scripture in Spiritual Formation* (Nashville, TN: Upper Room Books, 2000), chapter 2, "How to 'Read' without 'Reading.'"

to the text, our interaction with the text, and the impact of the text upon our lives.

This way of reading undermines *lectio*. It is but one facet of a whole mode of self-focused being that subverts genuine spiritual formation. For the purpose of spiritual formation, we do not approach scripture primarily as a body of information; nor do we bring to it mere techniques, methods, or models of formation. Rather we bring to the Word a different mode of being. Consider experimenting with this alternative as you read these chapters, especially as you begin to practice *lectio*, both individually and together in your Companions group.

First, our top priority is to listen for God. We try to focus on what God is saying to each of us personally as we read. We listen for God to speak to us in and through, around and above, behind and beneath the passage we are reading. We keep asking ourselves, "What is God trying to say to me in this passage?" With this posture toward the text, we begin to reverse the learned habit that establishes us as the controlling power that masters a body of information. Instead, we start allowing the text to become a place of God's encounter with us. We open to the possibility of God transforming our life through the text. Not only does this exercise shift our approach to reading and position us for *lectio*, it begins to transform our whole mode of being in a way that makes authentic spiritual formation possible.

Second, we begin to respond to what we read with our heart and spirit rather than with our rational intellect. We face no danger of neglecting the cognitive, analytical parts of our mind, which are hyperdeveloped in our culture and education. Indeed, we tend to be overbalanced in their direction, imagining that the sharper we are intellectually and the more quickly we grasp and integrate concepts, the more balanced we are! This is not wholeness of being. Yes, we are called to love God with our entire mind, to use the gifts of intellect and reason to the best of our ability. But in the Bible, loving God with all our heart and all our soul precedes loving God with our entire mind.[2]

> *How do we read in a way that allows us to be encountered by the Reality within yet beyond these familiar words?*
>
> —Marjorie J. Thompson

---

2. See Matthew 22:37; Mark 12:30; Luke 10:27; Jesus draws on Hebrew scriptures (Deut. 6:5).

The problem with imbalance among heart, soul, and mind is that our dominant emphasis on the mind allows us to stand back from the text, to be independent of it, to evaluate it in the light of our own best judgment and decide how we want to deal with it. Can you see the problem that arises here as we approach the Word-become-text? God desires to meet us in the text. Suppose we stand back in a purely rational manner, evaluate the text by our best reasoning—even enlightened Christian reasoning—and then determine that what we are reading is not for us. We choose to insulate ourselves against a transforming encounter with God. We do not open our being at deeper levels to the possibility of the Holy One meeting us in the text. We may respond to the passage, but often our response is simply that of reading ourselves into the text in some way rather than allowing God to speak to us out of it. How easily we can manipulate scripture to reinforce our "false self"—the structure of our self-focused being; and how readily we resist God's call to our "true self"—the person-hood that comes to life in being freely abandoned to God! Some of us may find it difficult to adopt this alternative way of reading. We may find ourselves leaning toward the cognitive, critical approach to the text. Yet *The Way of Scripture* invites us to give these suggestions a try. They will bear fruit with practice.

Third, as we practice *lectio*, we respond from deeper levels of our being. We ask ourselves questions like these: How do I feel about what is being said? Where do these words touch me? What images are evoked? How do I respond deep within? When we come to the second step of this way of reading—*meditatio*—we will begin to probe our initial responses through further questions: Why do I feel this way? What associations do I have with these words or images? Why am I responding in this way? What is going on within me? How is God encountering me in this text with challenge or invitation?

I want to encourage us to develop a mode of responding to the Word-become-text that allows it to become a place of transforming encounter with God. This mode of response helps us open up the "rational filter" by which we block much of God's voice. We can then begin to hear at the level of heart and soul. Jesus frequently reminded

The ancients realized that scripture, when read the right way, opens doors to a direct relationship with God. They discovered the prayer of sacred reading.

—Daniel Wolpert

Sacred reading is a living conversation between you and God.

—Daniel Wolpert

"those who had ears" to *hear*,[3] a strange exhortation unless it implied a hearing failure of some sort. I suspect that Jesus was talking about the operation of the "rational filter" by which the false self protects itself from transforming encounter with God.

Our culture forms us in such a way that we have ears to hear but do not hear. We don't know how to hear with the deeper levels of our being. Yet we need to rediscover this skill if we are going to allow the Word-become-text to transform us. Perhaps our greatest challenge will be learning a way to engage scripture that allows the Spirit to address us at deeper levels of our being through biblical words, images, and metaphors.

Learning to Practice Lectio

The first step of *lectio* unfolds like this: As you sink into the text and allow the Word to draw you out of yourself into its depths, be sensitive to what is going on within you. When a certain word or phrase stirs some feeling within, simply note it. You might have a pad and pen handy to record your experience at various points in the passage. Remember Merton's assertion that the Bible's nature is to insult, puzzle, and amaze the human mind. So the reader who opens the Bible must be prepared for disorientation, confusion, incomprehension, perhaps outrage. If you experience the text as an affront to some aspect of your life, note the verse, phrase, or word that triggered your response and name your reaction—anger, fear, anxiety, grief, guilt. Record where you find yourself disoriented, perplexed, irritated, or astonished. Something in the passage may delight, amaze, or elate you. Signify where this occurs as well. In a nutshell, watch with care how the Word-made-text becomes a place of encounter with God. Be alert to these inner movements in your mind, heart, and spirit. Try to name them without interpreting them. In the next stage of the process—*meditatio*—you will begin to wrestle with the nature and meaning of God's encounter with you in the Word.

We are doing more than reading words. . . . We are listening with the heart to the Holy within.

—Richard J. Foster

---

3. See Mark 4:9, 23; 8:18; Luke 14:35.

The practice of *lectio* promotes the use of the Ignatian method[4] of engaging our imagination while reading the text. Ignatius urged his disciples to place themselves into the setting of the passage. This is not always possible. It is unlikely that we can imagine ourselves in a particular location while reading Paul's letter to the Romans, for example, or the codes of Leviticus. However, where the text describes place and personal interaction, we can employ imagination to place ourselves in the setting and "read" it from within. The Ignatian method works best with narratives in scripture, such as the stories of Jesus' life and teachings recorded in the Gospels.

Suppose we consider the account where Jesus comes to the disciples as they struggle to cross the Sea of Galilee in the middle of a stormy night (Mark 6:47-52). In order to locate ourselves in the story, we need to explore the events leading up to this account (see Mark 6:7-46). Let's try identifying imaginatively with the disciples here. Jesus has sent us out on a mission to proclaim the kingdom and heal the sick. We return from the mission excited but weary, and Jesus issues an invitation to retreat: "Come away by yourselves to a deserted place and relax a bit." Imagine how we would feel—glad to have an opportunity to be alone with Jesus, to rest and be refreshed after our labors!

We get into a boat and sail away to a deserted spot; but when we arrive, instead of quiet retreat we find a crowd. Imagine how we feel then. So much for our quiet, relaxing time with Jesus! As evening falls after Jesus has taught the crowd for quite a while, we ask Jesus to dismiss the people. We want to begin our retreat. But instead of sending the crowd away, Jesus puts us to work serving a sit-down dinner for five thousand and cleaning up afterward. Finally, Jesus dismisses the crowd. But instead of beginning our retreat, he tells us to get into the boat and sail across to Bethsaida. So much for the retreat!

Now our story gets worse: we find ourselves fighting an adverse wind all night as we try to cross the Sea of Galilee. As one of the twelve disciples, I'm totally worn out—discouraged at missing our retreat

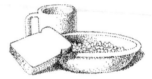

---

4. Ignatius of Loyola was a sixteenth-century Roman Catholic reformer best known for developing carefully structured spiritual exercises. The use of imagination to enliven one's encounter with God was one of his distinctive gifts to the church universal.

time, frustrated by this storm, my heart hardened. Then I look up and, to my horror, see what looks like a ghost approaching us on the water. Screaming in terror, I think, *This is the perfectly horrible end to a perfectly horrible day!* Then I hear the ghost say, in Jesus' voice, "Cheer up, it is I, don't be afraid." At first I feel confused, uncertain—*could this really be Jesus?* Then I feel immense relief—*it's not a ghost after all but my Teacher!* Finally, a sense of awe overwhelms me—*this man can walk across waves as if on dry land!* It makes the hairs on my neck stand straight up.

We are desiring to see, to hear, to touch the biblical narrative.

—Richard J. Foster

Do you see how reading the story from within opens it up in new ways? Here is an example of how we might enter into *lectio*. In Mark's Gospel we find the following account (8:22-26).

> Jesus and the disciples came into Bethsaida. They brought a blind man to Jesus demanding[5] that he touch him. Having taken the blind man's hand, Jesus led him out of the village. Then, having spit in the man's eyes and having laid his hands upon him, Jesus asked, "Do you see anything?" Having looked up, the man said, "I see people, but I see them like trees walking." Then Jesus laid his hands upon the man's eyes again. The man looked intently, and he was restored and was seeing everything clearly. Jesus sent the man home, saying, "Do not even enter the village."

To balance the rational and the feeling sides of *lectio*, we need to understand the situation of the text. Bringing an "informed imagination" to the story can help at this point. Bethsaida is an interesting village in the Gospels. It was the hometown of Philip, Peter, and Andrew (John 1:44; 12:21). Bethsaida was also a village where many of Jesus' mighty works of healing and feeding had been done (Luke 9:10-17). Strangely, however, Bethsaida had apparently rejected Jesus and his ministry (Matt. 11:21). After instructing the disciples on how to respond to a town that rejects them and their proclamation of the kingdom (Luke 10:10-12), Jesus says, "Woe to you, Chorazin; woe to you, Bethsaida; because if the mighty deeds which took place in you

---

5. The Greek term is usually translated "asked," "begged," or "exhorted." However, in the negative context of this account, "demanded" conveys more the tone of the request.

had taken place in Tyre and Sidon they would have repented long ago sitting in sackcloth and ashes. They will be better off in the judgment than you" (Luke 10:13-14). That two Gentile cities would receive better treatment in the judgment than two Jewish towns is a stark condemnation of Chorazin and Bethsaida's rejection of Jesus.

So when Jesus and the disciples come to Bethsaida, they enter hostile territory. This probably explains Jesus' unusual procedure of taking the blind man out of the village. In only one other instance in the Gospels does Jesus take a person away from his context to minister to him.[6] Perhaps Jesus takes the blind man out of the toxic atmosphere of a village that rejects Jesus' ministry. This interpretation may also explain Jesus' seemingly impossible command to the man when he sends him home saying, "Do not even enter the village." How can the man go to his home in the village without entering it? Does he live outside the village, or is Jesus suggesting that he not enter the toxic atmosphere of rejecting Christ and his ministry?

These factors can helpfully inform our understanding of this account. The concern of those who bring the man to Jesus does not center on the blindness but rather in putting Jesus to the test. Note that they even tell Jesus how to perform the healing—demanding that Jesus *touch* the man. With this understanding of the story's context, we are now prepared to enter into *lectio* with it. The Ignatian method of imagining oneself in the story works well with the text. I will illustrate the way I might imagine myself as the blind man to give you one possible way to hear the story "from within."

My Experience of Lectio with the Blind Man of Bethsaida

First, I set the stage for myself as the blind man. I imagine myself getting up this morning, performing my morning prayers, eating

---

6. This story is also in Mark (7:33) and has several characteristics of the account in Bethsaida. Jesus is in Gentile territory (the Decapolis) where it might be expected that a wandering Jewish teacher would be suspect or discounted. A group of people bring the needy man to Jesus, telling him how to heal the man and demanding that Jesus lay his hand upon him. Jesus takes the man away from the seemingly toxic situation in order to heal him.

my breakfast, setting out with my begging bowl to assume my place in the village square. There the Jewish townsfolk come for their daily supplies and, in obedience to the Torah, might be expected to give me alms.[7] I imagine sitting in my usual place, enjoying the cool of the morning before midday heat begins to build. I listen to the sounds of people going about their business in the town square: customers haggling with merchants, merchants hawking their wares, people in animated conversation, an argument breaking out. I smell the aromas of the town square: fresh fish just brought in to market,[8] the enticing smell of the bakery, the body odors of people passing by. I feel sun on my face and the warmth of the ground where I sit.

We begin to enter the story and make it our own. We move from detached observation to active participation.
—Richard J. Foster

Now I imagine hearing a group of people crossing the square, deep in discussion. As they draw nearer, my blindness-heightened sensitivity tells me they are coming directly to me. Instead of giving alms or striking up conversation with me, they stand me up and guide me across the square. I'm not sure how I feel about this. I'm a little encouraged by the attention but also anxious and uncertain. *Where are they taking me, and why?* They have given no explanation. *Should I ask or stay silent?*

I sense they have brought me to a person who stands before me. I hear them say in a confrontational tone, "Touch him. Let's see you heal this one." Now I'm starting to feel uncomfortable. I think I'm being used, and I don't like it. But they are talking about healing. *Is this person I'm standing before really a healer? Wouldn't it be amazing if he were and if he could actually heal me, a blind man?* But maybe he's a charlatan. They seem to be challenging him to prove he can do it. I'm probably the ultimate test. *Do I dare to hope?* My gut starts to churn.

Now the man they have brought me to takes my hand and starts to lead me away—out of the village. I hear the voices fading behind us. *Is this some cruel game being played on me? Is this man going to take me into the surrounding area and abandon me?* I know my way

---

7. For illustrations of the significance of giving alms, see Matthew 6:2-4; Luke 12:33; and Acts 3:2-3; 10:2, 31.

8. Fishing was generally done at night. See Luke 5:5 and John 21:3.

around the village, but out here I am lost. The sounds, smells, and things I touch for orientation are gone. I am being taken completely out of my comfort zone, and I'm starting to panic. *What is this man doing? Why is he taking me so far from everything I know? Who will help me get home? Why is this happening to me?* I'm feeling anxious.

Going from bad to worse, this man who has dragged me out here now spits in my face—an act of utter contempt. I am being demeaned, degraded. I want to weep with humiliation and rage. *Why am I being treated this way?* I want to run away, but I am helpless. I want to shout for help, but who is around us to hear?

Now this man places his hands on my eyes and asks, "Do you see anything?" What a stupid question! Not only am I blind, but I have his spittle coating my eyes. Yet as I wipe away the spittle and open my eyes, I realize I am seeing! Things are not very clear; people look like trees walking, but I am seeing! I'm totally shocked. Suddenly everything feels entirely different. Instead of feeling manipulated, humiliated, and helpless, a great surge of hope wells up in me. I become aware of the gentleness of this man's voice and hands. I realize that I couldn't feel his kind manner before because of my anxiety and anger.

The man places his hands on my eyes again, and now I am eagerly, expectantly cooperating with him. How much I want to be completely healed, to be able to see clearly ! Now I believe this man can actually heal me. I am amazed and completely receptive to what he is doing. I think my heart will burst with anticipation.

Now as I open my eyes again, I see everything clearly! I have been healed! Utter joy and amazement well up from deep within me. I look straight into my healer's face. It is beautiful—grave, intent, yet warm. His eyes are full of light. He exudes love. I know that he is a man of God and that God has touched me through him. My heart fills with gratitude beyond words. I want to go to the synagogue and make a sacrifice of praise and thanksgiving!

Yet my healer tells me, "Go home, but don't even enter the village." What is he saying? My home is in the village. How can I make a thank offering to God if I can't go to the synagogue in the village? I wonder what he means. I feel confused and uncertain.

Lectio divina is reading that is tasteful and relished. It is to savor the Word, to savor God.
—García M. Colombás

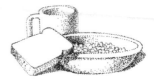

51

This is but one example of how we might experience the first step of *lectio*. At this point we do not concern ourselves with pondering answers to our questions or processing our feelings. This will come in the next stage—*meditatio*. During *lectio* simply take note of how the passage touches you and the nature of your feelings and images as you experience them. As you can see, in *lectio* you stay with a small portion of text, here only five verses. You read yourself into the text and allow the text to read itself into your life.

Practical Matters

What is the best way to select passages for the discipline of *lectio divina*? Some find the weekly lectionary helpful.[9] Over the course of three years, the lectionary covers much of the Bible. Lectionary readings are often short, self-contained units of text, which makes them ideal for *lectio*. The lectionary also simplifies our task by taking responsibility for selecting the passages. Another option is to work through a book of the Bible over an extended period. This approach has the advantage of allowing us to develop the context of the book before we begin so we can better read the text from "inside" as we work with each passage. Left to ourselves, we often stick to passages that are "comfortable," texts that do not confront or challenge us. Then it is difficult for the Word to become a place of transforming encounter with God. Whatever means you use to select texts, be sure that over a period of time you cover both Old and New Testament passages, taking care to explore all the major books and letters of each Testament.

Finally, it is good if possible to have a time and place devoted to the practice of *lectio*. Rather than give God "leftovers" of time, you can make this discipline a priority. Choose a time that will, as much as possible, be uninterrupted and open-ended so you do not have to stop a significant encounter with God midway. The place you choose

God actually speaks to us. Even more, God's heart is open to us and invites us to enter in, to scrutinize it, to get to know it.

—García M. Colombás

---

9. The lectionary is a systematized selection of scripture readings for public or private worship. Notice that "reading" is the common meaning for both *lectio* and lectionary.

for *lectio* needs to be one of minimal interruption—a comfortable place without distracting surroundings where you can commit to a focus upon meeting God in the Word-become-text.

Lectio works well with small groups and individuals. You will engage in group *lectio* often during these weeks with your companions in *The Way of Scripture*. In this case, the texts are selected for you, and the group meeting will allow for uninterrupted time and space to enter together into a deeper encounter with God in the Word-become-text. You will discover the blessing of listening more fully to the Spirit among you as you hear one another's responses to a Word that is still "living and active" (Heb. 4:12). May your ears be open!

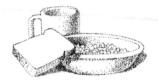

DAILY EXERCISES

Before starting these reflection exercises, read Week 3, "*Lectio*: Ingesting the Word." Record insights and questions in your journal. Continue journal entries as you reflect on the exercises below. We are starting the adventure of making connections between the great story of God's salvation and the little stories of our personal lives! Keep your favorite Bible at hand to check the larger context of the passages you are reading. Take time to pray for an open mind and heart, receptive to the gifts of the Holy Spirit.

EXERCISE 1

Read Matthew 22:34-40. Three of four Gospels record Jesus teaching this "greatest commandment." Its familiarity may blind us to the depth of its challenge in our lives.

Draw three columns down a page in your journal. Put the words *Heart, Soul,* and *Mind* across the top, heading each column. Under each word, think on paper what it means to love God with all your heart, soul, and mind. Note in each column ways you already feel or express your love for God. Put a star beside the dimension in you that seems strongest in love of God; draw a heart by the dimension that seems strongest in love of neighbor.

Try to identify the lens through which you relate most easily to God: feeling, intellect, will, or intuition. Choose to live the next twenty-four hours from a less familiar mode. For example, if your lens is feeling, try will; or if intellect, try feeling. Aim to bring this alternate faculty into your prayers, tasks, and encounters. Pay attention to any changes you notice as you broaden your scope.

EXERCISE 2

Read Mark 4:35-41. This story may connect with some of your fears or questions of faith. Practice *lectio* with this passage in the way the author suggests, alert to the movements within in your mind, heart, and spirit.

Read the text again, listening for the words or phrases that especially stir you. Note these in your journal without interpretation.

Now sink deeper into the story, placing yourself imaginatively in its setting and among its characters. Pay attention to thoughts and feelings that surface. Where do you find yourself anxious, irritated, astonished? Don't ask why or seek the meaning of your responses. Just observe and note them in your journal. You are practicing the *lectio* phase that precedes *meditatio*.

Give thanks to God for the way scripture opens to you something of your own experience, as well as something beyond it. Pray for grace to go deeper in God's time.

EXERCISE 3

Read Matthew 15:21-28. This text may elicit some of the uncomfortable feelings that Merton describes. As you reread the passage, notice any parts of the story that affront you. Name the feelings that surface for you as an observer.

Now enter the story imaginatively, identifying with the Canaanite woman. Where is the affront in Jesus' actions or words for you? Play out the story in your imagination, attending to the thoughts, feelings, and desires that transpire in your mother-heart. Tell this story in your journal the way our author tells the story of the blind man healed by Jesus. (Stay with feelings and images rather than moving to interpretation or meaning.)

Notice if your feelings as an observing reader and your feelings as the mother differ and, if so, how. Breathe thanks for any insights.

EXERCISE 4

Read Psalm 63. This psalm gathers several common human emotions into a single prayer. How many different moods of prayer can you identify in it?

As you slowly read this psalm again, what parts especially touch you? Note in your journal words and phrases that catch your attention. How do you feel about these words?

What images do these particular words and phrases evoke in you? Sketch a few of these images in symbolic ways in your journal. Then let them guide you into a time of prayer. If any of these images remind you of a song or hymn, sing or hum it as part of your prayer.

EXERCISE 5

Read Mark 14:3-9. The story of the woman anointing Jesus with ointment before his death is lavish in many ways. For *lectio* practice, it offers rich sensory images.

Read this story slowly "from within," imagining yourself present in the room as a guest. Bring a full sensory imagination to the story. What do you see, hear, taste, smell, and touch as you progress through the scene? Note these in your journal. Now imagine the story from the woman's position, including your feelings and senses. Finally imagine it from Jesus' perspective, allowing yourself to receive and enjoy this beautiful gift of anointing. Remember to avoid interpretations and meanings, focusing only on images, senses, and feelings.

Find a fragrance you enjoy (small tube of hand cream, a guest soap, cologne sprayed on a piece of paper). Place it in your pocket or purse as a reminder to attend to your senses as a possible means of grace in daily life.

Review the week's journal entries in preparation for the group meeting.

Week 4

Meditatio: Wrestling with God

In your practice of the *lectio* phase of spiritual reading, you responded to the text in the deeper levels of your being by posing questions such as these: "How do I feel about what is being said or done? How do I react on the surface? How do I respond deep within?"

As we come to the next phase, *meditatio* or meditation, we begin to process our questions more fully: "*Why* do I feel this way? *Where* are my reactions coming from? *What* is going on in my mind and heart? *How* is God encountering me here? *What* is the Holy Spirit stirring in my life?"

Meditatio provides an opportunity to tap into the deeper dynamics of our being by helping us explore inner terrain. What do my reactions to the Word-become-text tell me about my habits, attitudes, and perspectives in life? What do my responses reveal about my relationships with others or how I view myself? Through *meditatio* we gain a knowledge of ourselves that leads to God. We learn to balance our cognitive, rational responses to scripture by risking an affective, feeling response deep within.

Meditatio moves us from our modern informational approach to a much more ancient formational approach to scripture.[1] The

---

1. The following is adapted from my book, *Shaped by the Word*, chapter 5, "Information Versus Formation," 49–63.

formational way has been carried forward for centuries through Christian monasticism. The monastic writer Aelred Squire quotes William of Saint Thierry, a twelfth-century Cistercian abbott:

> The Scriptures need to be read in the same spirit in which they were written, and only in that spirit are they to be understood. You will never reach an understanding of Paul until, by close attention to reading him and the application of continual reflection, you imbibe his spirit. You will never arrive at understanding David until by the actual experience you realize what the psalms are about. And so it is with the rest. In every piece of Scripture, real attention is as different from mere reading as friendship is from entertainment, or the love of a friend from a casual greeting.

Squire then adds:

> If, in our own day, we are to do "holy reading" in the traditional sense of that phrase, nothing but conscious choice and the development of conscious habits of attention will be likely to cure us of a dissipation of mind that so much that we see and hear is designed to foster. As William of St Thierry goes on to point out, it is less what one reads than how one reads it that counts. It is an attitude of mind that is at issue.[2]

"An attitude of mind" is precisely the difference between the informational and formational approaches to scripture. An informational mentality, which in turn serves our functional bias, largely shapes our culture. We tend to seek more and more information—new facts, new bodies of knowledge, new techniques and methods, new systems and programs—in order to improve functional control over our environment. Acquiring information, techniques, and systems has little to do with enhancing the quality of our deeper being. It rather strengthens our ability to function in ways that allow us to shape the world to our liking. So the informational mentality of our culture closely companions our functional aims.

Whereas the study of Scripture centers on exegesis, the meditation upon Scripture centers on internalizing and personalizing the passage. The written Word becomes a living word addressed to us.

—Richard J. Foster

---

2. Aelred Squire, *Asking the Fathers: The Art of Meditation and Prayer* (New York: Paulist Press/Wilton, CT: Morehouse-Barlow, 1976), 124–25.

The dynamics of information-function are deeply ingrained in the fabric of our culture. They create one of those binding and blinding perceptions that take over automatically when we read. We have been trained to read informationally. Here are some characteristics of this way of reading:

- Informational reading seeks to cover as much as possible as quickly as possible. One of the ill effects of this approach is seen in programs designed to read the entire Bible in a brief period of time, such as a year.

- Informational reading is linear. We move from the first element to the second to the third, and so on to the end, thinking that reading is little more than the process of moving sequentially through a text.

- Informational reading seeks to master the text. We want to grasp it, to "get our minds around it." In this way, we bring it under our control, interpreting the text based on information we have already mastered. Then we typically seek to justify our interpretation and defend it against other interpretations.

- With informational reading the text is an object "out there" for us to manipulate according to our own intentions or desires. We keep ourselves at an objective distance from the text, an approach that pervades our whole educational process.

- This approach is analytical, critical, and judging—a natural outcome of standing back and running what we read through the filters of our own categories and perceptions. It is a cognitive, intellectual approach.

- Finally, informational reading tends toward problem solving. This feeds back into our functional way of being. We often read to find out *how* something can work for us. Just as we read the instruction manual for a piece of equipment that isn't working properly, we can read scripture mainly to find solutions to areas of our spiritual life that we think need "fixing." Then we reduce God's living Word to an instruction manual for rules of right living.

Please do not infer here that the informational approach is unnecessary or inferior to the formational where scripture is concerned. Informational reading is helpful in its proper context. Merton offers a good summary of the interplay between the informational and formational modes: "This [engagement with the biblical text] . . . requires two levels of understanding: first, a preliminary unravelling of the meaning of the texts themselves . . . which is mainly a matter of knowledge acquired by study."[3] This is the informational dynamic, and Merton rightly stresses its importance. If you recall our *lectio* on the blind man of Bethsaida, we needed a "preliminary unraveling" of the context before engaging the story as we did. But there is, Merton continues, "a deeper level, a living insight which grows out of personal involvement and relatedness. . . . Only on this second level is the Bible really grasped."[4] *Meditatio* takes us to the second level.

We need a certain interplay between the informational and formational modes of spiritual reading. But Merton sets it straight: the informational approach is only the "front porch" of our engagement with the Bible. Once we have crossed the porch, we enter that deeper encounter with the Word through the formational process of *meditatio*. Here, as the inner posture of our being shifts, we can become receptive, responsive listeners. Then God gains access to us for a transforming encounter.

We have, however, a strong tendency to approach even *meditatio* informationally. For many of us, this approach is unconscious and habitual. Some of us may reflect on scripture primarily to master words and ideas, to determine whether we can use them to get what we seek in our spiritual lives. If this is so, where is the space—the silence—in which God can speak? How can the Word-become-text be a place of transforming encounter with God?

Merton provides a corrective for our habitual approach to *meditatio* in reminding us that serious Bible reading grows out of *personal involvement* rather than mere intellectual assent (see quote above). When we read for information, we may inwardly agree or disagree with

> *Through meditation we establish in our spirit a space where the Word of God can echo.*
>
> —García M. Colombás

---

3. Merton, *Opening the Bible*, 61.
4. Ibid., 61–62.

ideas; but we do not tend to involve ourselves intimately, openly, receptively in what we read. This level of engagement may feel too dangerous or threatening. Yet *meditatio* calls us to precisely such personal involvement with the text. It calls us to let the text probe deeply into our lives—to illumine dark corners, challenge entrenched assumptions, confront false values, heal damaged emotions/memories, and repair the destructive dynamics of our way of life.

The formational approach to reading offers a very different pattern from our normal informational posture. Here are some of the balancing characteristics of formational reading:

- In formational reading our concern is less with completing long passages quickly as though it were an assignment and more with focusing on small portions of text. We may find ourselves holding in mind just one word or phrase, one sentence or paragraph. The object is not to complete the passage but to allow it to be a place of encounter with God. Some of us may be arguing inside right now: "I have this text before me. I've got to get through it, to understand it and move on." But spiritual reading invites us to freedom, freedom to reflect and meditate on deeper levels of God's presence in a passage. We give ourselves permission to slow down and sink into the Word-become-text.

- While informational reading is linear, formational reading goes to depth. We allow the passage to open us to its multiple layers of meaning. For the Word to be a place of encounter with God, we need to move deeper and deeper into the text. We learn to let the passage become an intrusion of God's Word into our life, addressing us for the sake of our spiritual transformation. An illustration may help. Suppose I see a man coming toward me. I start walking toward him talking steadily as I approach. I shake his hand and continue talking the whole time. Of course, he has no chance to address me. This is often what we do with scripture. We open to a passage, and our minds immediately begin to inform it. We go through the entire text and tell it what we think it says. Then we judge it: "That was a great passage" or "That didn't say

In our personal meditation we confine ourselves to a brief selected text, which possibly may not be changed for a whole week.

—Dietrich Bonhoeffer

How hard to communicate a message to one wielding a leaf blower!

—Norvene Vest

a thing to me." The text never has a chance to address us on its own terms!

- In formational reading, instead of trying to master the text, we allow it to master us. We come to the Bible open to hear, receive, and respond—to be a servant of the Word rather than a master of the text. The text becomes the subject of our relationship instead of an object we manipulate through our interpretation. We are the object being shaped by the Word. We willingly place ourselves before the text and await its address, ready for the Word-become-text to exercise influence over us. *Meditatio* requires patient waiting before the text, taking time to hear God speak to us through it.

- Instead of the analytical, critical approach, formational reading needs a humble, loving approach. This tall order requires a reorientation of our inner posture. We can slow down the pace of our process; probe more deeply into the text, even begin to see the text as addressing us—all with no radical shift of our perceptions or basic posture of being. We simply make some adjustments to our informational mind-set. However, when we become genuinely open and receptive to the Word, yielded to a penetrating encounter with God that confronts our false and distorted self, then we discover our need for more than minor adjustments to the status quo. Here we begin to hear the call of God to a deeper relationship, one that allows the Word to become flesh in us.

- Finally, in contrast to the problem-solving mentality of informational reading, *meditatio* remains open to mystery. Instead of coming to the text to find a solution for an unresolved issue in our life, we come and open ourselves to the Mystery we call God. We stand before this Mystery and allow it to address us. We may eventually discover that practical benefits emerge from this meeting, but we do not enter the meeting to get such results. In spiritual reading we practice letting go, releasing our agendas to God.

We need to guard against our habitual tendencies at this point. We are such subtle beings; we can let the old self-oriented mentality sneak unnoticed in the backdoor or side window after closing and

Often we shall have to stop with one sentence or even one word, because we have been gripped and arrested and cannot evade it any longer.

—Dietrich Bonhoeffer

barring the front door! Again and again we may find ourselves slipping back into an informational way of reading because it is self-protective. When the Word really begins to address us, our first impulse may be a retreat to the informational mode. We are generally more comfortable being the "master," controlling the text and thus limiting its influence on our life. Genuine transformation is scary and difficult, especially when the Word addresses us at a particularly painful point in our spiritual condition. We can resist the temptation to flee back to an informational control of the text by praying, "Lord, what are you saying to me in this passage?" or "Help me to hear your Word without fear, O God."

Perhaps now we can begin to see how this formational approach to scripture is a discipline that needs to be developed. Most of us race through our years frantically trying to maintain precarious control of the speeding vehicle of our life. We crave time to slow down and let go of control. Relaxation prepares our inner spirit for formational reading and meditation. The preparation itself is spiritually forming! Just coming to the point where we can absorb scripture in a formational way is already a tremendous step in spiritual growth. Even if there seems to be no encounter with God in a particular text on a particular day, the steady practice of preparing ourselves inwardly and entering into *meditatio* is itself spiritually forming.

An Example of Group Meditatio

Here is the experience of participants in a class I taught at the college of a denomination that does not allow women to serve in a pastoral role. I asked them to go off individually and use the story of Mary and Martha (Luke 10:38-42) for an experience of *lectio divina*. After about an hour, the class reassembled, and I asked for persons willing to share how God had encountered them in the passage. At first there was "safe" sharing, acknowledging the predominance of "Martha-ness" in their lives. Then one of the women courageously related her encounter with God. She had been a missionary with this denomination and in her responsibilities as a missionary had been

allowed to serve pastoral roles. She said she had been allowed to be "Mary," sitting at Jesus' feet, as it were, to be nurtured for pastoral service. With tears running down her face, she said that now that she was back in the States, she had been relegated to the role of "Martha," demoted to the kitchen to fulfill a woman's role in the church.

This woman's daring transparency emboldened other women in the class to open up and speak of similar experiences with this passage. Then one of the male pastors in the class stood and, with deep emotion, expressed his repentance and remorse for his contribution to this state of affairs in the denomination. He admitted that he had viewed women as "Marthas" and pastors as "Marys." His witness opened the entire class to a group *meditatio* in which they began to wrestle not only with how God was encountering them as individuals but also with how God was addressing them as a community of faith. *Meditatio* in turn led into a time of group *oratio* (we will discuss this in the next chapter) in which they poured out their hearts to God in contrition, repentance, and resolve to let this experience serve as God's transforming grace in their lives, personally and corporately.

This is what can happen when we engage in *meditatio* rather than traditional Bible study. *Meditatio* is more a formational than informational process. Through it we allow the Word-become-text to address us. God encounters us in divine freedom as we willingly take the posture of those addressed and reshaped by the Word.

> *Is not Sacred Scripture a letter from almighty God to creation? . . . I beg of you, apply yourself daily to meditating on the words of your Creator.* **Learn to know the heart of God in the words of God.**
>
> —Gregory the Great

An Example of Personal Meditatio

Let's return for a moment to the illustration of my *lectio* on the blind man of Bethsaida in chapter 3. At each step of that story I asked myself questions: *How do I feel about this? What is going through my mind? What is my gut reaction? What am I going to do?*

In the stage of *meditatio*, I now wrestle with what God is revealing to me in my answers to those questions. Like the blind man, I have become accustomed to my comfort zone. At times in my life, I too have been led out of familiar surroundings into unknown territory. *What is God revealing to me in my reaction to this discomfort as*

I role-play the blind man? Life sometimes spits in my face. *Is God telling me something through my gut reaction as I identify with the blind man in this kind of experience? When I open my eyes the first time and note something other than darkness, what is God saying to me in how I respond?* After a transforming experience, I have to return to my everyday life. *When Jesus tells me as the healed blind man to go home but not enter the village, does the Spirit reveal something to me about a new option in my own life?*

I hope we can see more clearly now how *meditatio* becomes a means of grace. It asks us to consider how a text challenges and invites us to grow spiritually beyond where we are. Through this reflective process God probes us, revealing things within that need attention, areas of our personhood that are not what they were created to be, aspects of our relationship with God that the Holy Spirit is seeking to transform, dynamics in our relationships with others that need to become more Christlike, dimensions of our life in the world that are called to become places of divine presence through us. In *meditatio* the Word-become-text truly becomes a place of transforming encounter with God.

Meditation is more effective when you involve several aspects of yourself—thinking, feeling, imagining, sensing.

—Marchiene Vroon
Rienstra

DAILY EXERCISES

Read Week 4, "*Meditatio*: Wrestling with God." Record insights, questions, and struggles in your journal. Now we are going deeper into the experience of God's active presence in the Word. Keeping your Bible at hand, continue journal entries with each exercise below. Pray for the courage and grace to allow God to encounter you in scripture in a way that leads to genuine transformation of your mind and heart.

EXERCISE 1

Read Matthew 13:13-16. Jesus knows that seeing and hearing do not always translate into true perception or understanding. Diligent searching and reflection are needed to comprehend the things of God. Aelred Squire (see page 58) speaks of a "dissipation of mind" our culture tends to foster. Reflect on your experience of scattered attention when you try to meditate or pray. Draw a line down the middle of a journal page. On the left side, list some ways that loss of focus finds expression in your life. On the right side, note cultural realities (technology, media; expectations from family, work, or self) that encourage this dissipation of mind.

Reread verses 14-15, and let them carry you into prayer. Ask the Spirit gently but clearly to reveal to you how your heart has grown dull, your ears hard of hearing, or your eyes unseeing. Respond to what you discover inwardly. Set an intention to be among the "blessed" whose eyes see and ears hear (v. 16).

EXERCISE 2

Read Psalm 42. In this psalm of yearning for God's felt presence and help in distress, many phrases may speak to your condition. One will serve as a frame for our meditation: *Deep calls to deep*. In the words of our author, "formational reading goes to depth" and "multiple layers of meaning."

Read the psalm again, paying attention to words or phrases that catch your inner ear (*lectio*). Note these in your journal. Select one word or phrase to ponder more fully, repeating it gently to yourself. Write down images, feelings, or memories associated with it. Now ask why this word or phrase seeks your attention at this moment in your life. What does the Spirit want to say to you? Where is the invitation to new growth? Allow this *meditatio* to become a "live encounter."

Come back to the phrase, *Deep calls to deep.* Where do you experience the resonance between God's Spirit and yours? Offer a prayer of thanks with gestures or movements that express the feelings of your heart before God.

EXERCISE 3

Return to Exercises 3 and 5 from last week, selecting the one you would like to carry into the *meditatio* stage of *lectio divina*. Reread the given text from either Matthew or Mark.

Refresh your memory of the feelings, senses, and images connected with the story. Then begin to move to meanings and interpretations. Open your heart to receptivity with words like, "Speak, LORD, your servant is listening" (1 Sam. 3:10). Ask God to help you discover responses to these questions: Why do I have these feelings? How do they connect with my life? What do they signify in my relationship with you, God? What would you have me pay attention to in the images that have surfaced? Where is your divine invitation to me in this story at this time?

Record in your journal any responses you discover. Allow an image to surface that expresses what it feels like to move from *lectio* to *meditatio*. Try sketching this image.

EXERCISE 4

Read Luke 10:38-42. You reflected on this passage two weeks ago. Come back to it now from a different angle to explore more layers of meaning. We want to consider how information can enrich and deepen formation.

Ponder the following points of information that scholars have helped us understand about this passage: Martha was doubtless the eldest in this household, since the text identifies the home as hers. She plays the traditional and expected role of a woman in that time.

Mary is portrayed in terms that refer to a disciple: she sat at Jesus' feet to receive religious teaching, a position reserved for the men and boys in her culture.

Practice *lectio* and *meditatio* with this story, bringing an informed imagination to your reflection. What difference does the information make in your encounter and identification with the story's characters? How does your sense of Jesus' invitation to you deepen? Capture insights in your journal.

EXERCISE 5

Read Matthew 6:19-21. This teaching from Jesus' Sermon on the Mount challenges conventional thinking and practice, especially in a rich nation. Even if we are not personally wealthy, the challenge stands.

Practice the steps of *lectio* and *meditatio* with this teaching. Let the word or phrase that most speaks to you settle in your mind and heart. Repeat it gently, paying attention to associations, images, feelings, or memories that surface. Note them in your journal. Then ask how this word or phrase encounters you, where it connects with your life and what kind of resistance you feel to it. Where is your "treasure"? What is God's challenge or invitation to you? Note insights.

If you find yourself anxious, pray for help to hear and follow without fear. Then choose one way to act on this teaching today. Offer your act to God in a spirit of praise and thanksgiving.

Review the week's journal entries in preparation for the group meeting.

Week 5
Oratio: Letting God Know How We Feel

*O*ratio is Latin for "prayer." Once again, deeply ingrained assumptions may come into play when we hear the word *prayer*. We tend to think of prayer as something we *do*. Certainly prayer has a "doing" aspect. Yet our culture often overemphasizes performance to the neglect of an activity's deeper aspects. Paul's counsel to "pray without ceasing" (1 Thess. 5:17) alerts us to the depth dimension. Is Paul simply speaking in hyperbole to stress the importance of prayer? Surely he knows that we need to sleep, eat, earn a living, and deal with daily relationships. How can Paul call us to pray without ceasing?

If we identify prayer largely with "doing," then we cannot do other things while we pray. Consequently, our ordinary life and our prayer become divided. Except for emergencies that compel us to pray in the heat of the moment, we usually step aside from daily activities to pray. Once we have prayed, we resume our normal tasks and relationships. But recall that a formational approach to scripture is less about our *doing* than our *being*. What if we apply this insight to prayer? Might Paul be calling us to a relationship with God that permeates our entire life?

Maybe Paul understands that prayer is to our being what breathing is to our body. Breathing is not an occasional activity we engage in when we have time and interest. It pervades every moment. We continually breathe. When exerting ourselves physically, we don't

Just as breathing goes on naturally within our bodies, our personal prayer of praise and petition plays in our mind and sings in our heart even when we are not focusing on it.

—Ron DelBene

stop breathing but rather breathe harder. Paul seems to be suggesting in his call to pray without ceasing that prayer is the "breath" of our being, vital to our spiritual existence.

Paul's letters speak of the dynamic nature of our relationship with God. Listen to Paul's prayer for the Ephesians and, by extension, for us. (I have added numbers after each "that" in the prayer so we can easily see and expand on his points):

> I pray that, (1) according to the riches of God's very nature,[1] you may be strengthened with power through God's Spirit in your inner being; that (2) Christ may dwell in your hearts through faith; I pray that (3) as you are being rooted and grounded in love you may have the power to comprehend, with all the saints, what is the breadth and length and height and depth, in other words[2] to know the love of Christ that surpasses knowledge; that (4) you may be filled with all the fullness of God (3:16-19).

Paul intends this prayer for all believers, not just for the spiritual elite. Notice the profoundly intimate nature of the relationship he prays for believers to have with God. Paul is not engaging in theological discussion here; he is describing the essence of a believer's relationship with God. Let's explore the four clauses of this prayer.

First, believers are to be "strengthened with power" through the presence of God's Spirit in their "inner being."[3] One dimension of the deepest nature of believers—their being—is that they are persons indwelt by the divine Spirit.

Second, Paul says Christ is to "dwell" in their hearts, using the same term he uses to describe God's dwelling in Jesus.[4] Here is another dimension of the essential being of believers—they are persons in whom Christ dwells as a living reality.

---

1. In Greek, "his glory." See the discussion of "glory" in chapter 1.
2. The structure of this sentence indicates that "to know the love of Christ" is "to comprehend with all the saints what is the breadth, length, height, and depth."
3. The Greek literally means the "inner" or "inmost man." This is the term Paul uses in 2 Corinthians 4:16 where he says our inner being is being renewed daily, and in Romans 7:22 where he says he delights in the law of God in his inmost being.
4. Colossians 1:19; 2:9.

Third, Paul shows that this relationship is rooted and grounded in love by using the term *agape*, a radically other-centered love. Believers are grounded in God's agape, a cross-shaped love by which God reveals a heart of total self-giving for us. We in turn are rooted in a radically God-centered love, a cross-shaped love in which we lose ourselves for God's sake.[5] Here is a third dimension of the inner reality of believers: they are bonded with God in a mutual relationship of self-giving love.

Additionally, Paul says, those embedded in God's love experience a mystical relationship with Christ that defies rational comprehension: they "know the love of Christ that surpasses knowledge." Believers are drawn into a whole new realm of being, immersed in "the breadth and length and height and depth" of Christ's love.

Finally, in his boldest statement of all, Paul expects believers to be "filled with all the fullness of God." To be filled with the divine fullness implies an ongoing state of being, not an occasional moment of inspiration or ecstasy. This is the fourth and consummate dimension of the being reality of believers. Truly it defies imagination!

In Paul's prayer for the Ephesians we find the essence of *oratio* as well as the proper way to understand his call to pray without ceasing. In a life of such intimate union with God, prayer is the dynamic interplay of that union. Here is how Merton describes the relationship:

> Hard as it is to convey in human language, there is a very real and very recognizable . . . Presence of God, in which we confront Him in prayer knowing Him by Whom we are known, aware of Him Who is aware of us, loving Him by Whom we know ourselves to be loved. Present to ourselves in the fulness of our own personality, we are present to Him Who is infinite in His Being, His Otherness, His Self-hood. It is not a vision face to face, but a certain presence of self to Self in which, with the reverent attention of our whole being, we know Him in Whom all things have their being.[6]

In *lectio* and *meditatio* we have sought to allow the Word-become-text to be a place of transforming encounter with God. We have

---

5. Matthew 10:39.

6. Thomas Merton, *Thoughts in Solitude* (Boston: Shambhala Publications, 1993), 49.

opened ourselves to God in deep receptivity. Now in *oratio* we pour out our heart to God. *Oratio* is our inner response to the encounter with God. There is no set pattern, no special technique here—only the sharing of heart with Heart.

Recall the group experience with the Mary-Martha story in the previous chapter. The class members' *oratio* was a catharsis of grief, bitterness, and anger for the women; an outpouring of remorse, repentance, and resolve for the men. Each group saw themselves in a new light through their encounter with God in the passage. Often *oratio* will begin at such a point. We wrestle with what our encounter with God has revealed to us about ourselves. *Oratio* may continue over an extended period until we either reject or accept what was revealed in our encounter with God.

If we get to the point of acceptance, our prayer naturally becomes confession. We begin to agree with God about the nature of our condition. Then we can move from confession to a prayer of yielding ourselves to the transformation only God can bring about within us.

Prayer means nothing else but the readiness and willingness to receive and appropriate the Word, and . . . to accept it in one's personal situation, particular tasks, decisions, sins, and temptations.

—Dietrich Bonhoeffer

We see from this example that *oratio* may take the form of wrestling with God. It provides a way of becoming honest in response to the encounter God has initiated through the Word-become-text. At times, such prayer is a struggle with the conflict between our perception and God's perception of who we are. This surely must have been the case for the believers in Laodicea whom Jesus addresses in Revelation 3:14-22. Jesus first offers an image of the Laodicean believers' perception of themselves: "'I am rich, I have prospered, and I need nothing.'" It sounds like they really had it all together; the Laodicean church was settled and secure in its identity. We then see Jesus' perception of these believers: "'You are wretched, pitiable, poor, blind, and naked'" (3:17). There would certainly have been rich material for *meditatio* among the believers of Laodicea, and we might imagine their *oratio* moving from outrage to deep contrition.

Let's consider some other possible dynamics of *oratio*. A scripture passage might open hidden reservoirs of bitterness and resentment, some of which could be directed at God. We become resentful in situations where we feel we have been abandoned by God, bitter when we think the Almighty should have done something to help us. *Oratio* might take the form of screaming our rage at God. If that idea causes uneasiness or outright horror, it could be helpful to pray with a few psalms of lament (see 13; 22; 44; 88) or of "imprecation" (see 10; 69:16-29; 74; 79; 83). The imprecatory psalms call on God to rain down justice upon the enemy's head!

God can handle our anger. Indeed, our feelings are no surprise to the One who knows all things. There may be more genuine prayer in expressing our anger to God than in all our pious platitudes. Often, of course, we direct our bitterness and resentment at others—especially those who have injured or mistreated us, ridiculed or rejected us, used or abused us. The mere recollection of what they did or said stirs up anguish and anger. In such cases *oratio* may become a plea for God to help us begin the long, hard process of forgiving those who have wronged us. God knows that our inability to forgive is a cancer in our souls, eating away the vitality of our well-being. Through the Word-become-text, God probes these tender, wounded areas of our life. *Oratio* may then become a struggle to let God bring cleansing and healing to poisonous inner pockets of bitterness and resentment.

At times our encounter with God in scripture releases deep springs of joy. Some joy arises from situations where we realize how God is present with us in far richer ways than we had known or imagined. Other times joy simply wells up unbidden within us, from depths we cannot fathom. In such instances *oratio* may take expression in gales of laughter, tears of joy, or songs of praise and thanks to God. Our prayer might simply be a heartfelt "Yes! . . . Yes! . . . Yes!" You may have noticed that psalms of lament and even imprecation often resolve into thanks and praise. When we steep ourselves in the psalms, we find abundant words to express our response to God's grace and goodness: "I give you thanks, O Lord, with my whole heart" (138:1); "Bless the Lord, O my soul, and all that is within me, bless God's holy name" (103:1); "O give thanks to the Lord who is good, whose steadfast love endures forever" (136:1). Prayers of joy and thanksgiving lead us naturally into that deep sense of belonging and loving union that Paul prays we will come to know in all its fullness.

Sacred Scripture is Jacob's well, whence is drawn the water that immediately spills over into prayer.

—Arnold of Bohéries

Sometimes God encounters us in the Word in ways that bring a sense of foreboding. Tendrils of fear may entwine our thoughts and feelings. Our anxiety may relate to facing a significant decision, a difficult situation, or a challenging relationship. *Oratio* here might mean acknowledging our fear to God, seeking divine courage to face our fear, and wisdom to move through it entrusting ourselves to the Good Shepherd. Again, the psalms can provide words for our prayer: "Even though I walk through the darkest valley, I fear no evil; for you are with me" (23:4). We can personalize a psalm to make it our own address to God: "You, Lord, are my light and my salvation; whom shall I fear? You are the stronghold of my life; of whom shall I be afraid?" (27:1); or "God is my refuge and strength, a very present help in trouble. Therefore I will not fear, though the earth should change, though the mountains shake in the heart of the sea" (46:1-2).

At times, God confronts us in scripture in a way that perplexes us. For example, we may discover that "the good is the enemy of the best." Sometimes we get stuck in a rut of mere decency when God has something more in mind for us. God's encountering us in our reasonable goodness with a call to a higher path may generate bewilderment. *Oratio* may then become a wrestling match in which we try to convince God that our present approach to being or doing is fine, and we need not change. Our prayer may question God's wisdom in calling us to something unexpected. Yet if we desire to grow fully into divine grace, our prayer will become the yes of deep receptivity and obedience. Imagine Abraham's prayer when God called him to sacrifice his son Isaac (see Gen. 22:2). Isaac, a miracle child, was born to Abraham when he was one hundred and to Sarah who had been barren all her life. Moreover, Isaac fulfilled God's promise to Abraham, the one through whom his descendants would become as numerous as the stars of heaven (see Gen. 15:5). Surely God wouldn't want Abraham to sacrifice Isaac! If we can put ourselves in Abraham's shoes, we will glean some idea of the *oratio* of perplexity and incomprehension, yielding finally to the choice of acceptance and trust.

These few examples note how *oratio* might arise as we meet God through scripture. This form of prayer can be a dynamic dialogue

> Oratio *is the direct cry of the heart to God that rises when we have heard ourselves personally addressed through the Word.*
>
> —Marjorie J. Thompson

between yourself and the divine Self. At the heart of *oratio* is an encounter between who we now are and God's vision for who we are to become. The first movement of this prayer is often our reaction to what God is calling us to be or do. When expressed with openness and honesty, our reaction helps us see more clearly who we are and how we operate—to see ourselves as God sees us. This can lead us to accept God's view of us and admit that we are not all we are intended to be. The second movement of *oratio* is opening to God's purpose, entertaining an alternate way of being and doing. The final movement of this prayer is a willing and loving acceptance of God's purpose, a yielding of our will to God's, not in grudging acquiescence but in eager abandonment to God's life-giving love.

The process of *oratio* may continue over a period of time; you may not complete it in one session of *lectio divina*. This suggests that *lectio* does not require a different passage of scripture every day. We may find it important to stay with a passage for several days or even weeks, allowing God to develop the encounter with us to its fullest so it can culminate in life transformation.

Do you remember the image of prayer being to our souls what breathing is to our bodies? Just as our bodies live in an oxygen-rich environment, our souls exist in a Spirit-rich environment. God's presence envelops and indwells us. In this context, we think of *oratio* as breathing out the stale, fetid air of self-focused life and breathing in the fresh, revitalizing air of God's transforming Spirit. The catalyst for such breathing is our encounter with God in the Word-become-text.

"Divine reading" favors and enlivens the life of prayer.
—García M. Colombás

DAILY EXERCISES

Read Week 5, "*Oratio*: Letting God Know How We Feel." Record insights and struggles in your journal. Continue journal entries with these exercises, each of which is based on a psalm. As the prayer book of the Bible, the Psalms express every conceivable emotion and give us a wonderful opportunity to practice *oratio*. Pray for willingness to express your heart fully to God in prayer. Ask the Spirit to reveal dimensions of feeling you may not be fully aware of, so you can come to greater self-knowledge and bring more of yourself into conscious relationship with God's transforming grace.

EXERCISE 1

Read Psalm 51, focusing on verses 1-2, 10-12, and 15-17. Allow this classic psalm of penitence to carry you into a time of confession and contrition.

Begin by reflecting over the past week or so. Notice what you wish you could "take back" or do differently—perhaps words spoken rashly, unkind or judgmental thoughts, actions that wounded or embarrassed someone. What raises feelings of guilt or shame in you? Note these in your journal.

Where do you feel you most need God's help? Write your thoughts. Then listen for where God says you need the most help. Invite the Spirit to speak to your heart about change, cleansing, or healing. Write your own psalm of confession as your *oratio*.

EXERCISE 2

Read Psalm 44, a national psalm of lament and prayer. The lament begins with verse 9: Israel feels rejected by God and shamed before surrounding nations. While our context differs, we can surely identify with many of the feelings expressed here.

Read verses 9-26 again, paying attention to words or phrases that speak to you (*lectio*). Jot them down. Ponder how these words and feelings connect with your life experience (*meditatio*). When have you felt the sting of what seemed an unjustified punishment or a great hardship that made you wonder, *Why me?* When you believe you have been unfaithful to God, where do you take your feelings of anguish?

Enter into an *oratio* of lament. Don't be afraid to express the depth of your pain, grief, or anger. Remember that God knows and receives all our feelings into a heart of divine love. Write your lament in your journal. Listen for how God may respond inwardly.

EXERCISE 3

Read Psalm 46. This psalm has offered assurance and solace to countless generations of believers. Yet the terrors described here make our hearts shrink: earthquakes, nations collapsing, the desolations of war. What events in community, nation, or world have made you fearful recently? What decisions, situations, or relationships in your own life create anxiety? Express your fears to God in honest prayer. Write words or draw images in your journal that capture the essence of your *oratio*.

"Give to the winds thy fears," counsels one hymn. Find a phrase in Psalm 46 that helps calm your anxiety. Repeat this phrase inwardly for a few minutes. As you speak it inwardly or aloud, imagine casting into the wind of God's Spirit each fear you have noted. Let them all go. Breathe your thanks to the One who is forever our refuge.

EXERCISE 4

Read Psalm 137, a prayer of both lament and imprecation. Bitter lament can lead naturally to feelings of rage and may have done so in your *oratio* with Psalm 44 above.

Read verses 8-9 again. What depth of anguish might account for a desire to "pay you back" in this way? Imagine the feelings of Jews held captive for decades in a foreign land after the symbolic center of their nation and faith had been brutally destroyed.

Have you known a symbolic center of your nation or faith ruthlessly destroyed? What part of you weeps over the tactics of "enemies" who abuse power to cause harm? In what aspect of your personal life do you feel "captive" or "torn down"? Pay attention to your gut. What do you want to do to those you perceive as harming you or harming those you love? Draw an image in your journal of what you'd like to do. Then give yourself permission to write a psalm of imprecation. Notice what happens inside as you give your most difficult feelings to God. Listen deeply for where God is directing those feelings.

EXERCISE 5

Read Psalm 146, a psalm of pure praise for God's saving help, an affirmation that deeply answers every human cry of penitence, lament, fear, or revenge. Allow this psalm to carry your spirit into joyful praise.

Reread the psalm slowly, savoring phrases and images that speak to your heart. Find a phrase that captures your hope and trust in God. Repeat it inwardly for a time. Then ponder where you have known God's help in your life and the lives of your loved ones. Where have you experienced divine strength, freedom, vision, or watchful care? Note insights in your journal.

Recall a song or hymn that expresses your gratitude. Sing, hum, or listen to it in a spirit of deep joy! Carry the song with you through the remaining hours of the day and let it accompany you into sleep.

Review the week's journal entries in preparation for the group meeting.

Week 6
Contemplatio: Abandoning Ourselves to God in Love

*C*ontemplatio sounds a lot like the term *contemplation*. There is certainly a connection but not in the way we might think.

In ordinary English, contemplation is a type of mental activity. The dictionary defines it as "meditation on spiritual things" or the "act of considering with attention; musing; study."[1] We tend to see contemplation as concentrated mental activity. When we "contemplate" doing something, we think through possibilities, evaluate consequences, weigh factors, then come to a decision. But the spiritual meaning of contemplation differs greatly from this secular sense of the word, and the practice of *lectio divina* illustrates the difference.

In *lectio divina*, the stage of *contemplatio* is crucial to the transforming purpose of the process. Through *silentio* we reorient ourselves toward the Word-become-text, allowing it to become a place of divine encounter. In *lectio* we immerse ourselves in scripture, ingesting the text and receiving God's address to us through it. In *meditatio* we wrestle with ways the Word challenges, comforts, confirms, perplexes, or confuses us. In *oratio* we pour out our gut reaction or heartfelt response to how God is encountering us in the text. Then, in *contemplatio,* we allow this divine encounter to become transformative.

We practice *contemplatio* by becoming still before the mystery of God. This stillness is a deep inner quiet, a state of simply being in the

> Contemplation is essentially rest, play, Sabbath-time in God's presence
> —Marjorie J. Thompson

---

1. *Webster's New Collegiate Dictionary*, s.v. "contemplation."

presence of God. We find it difficult to attain such a simple state of being. Many of us have been estranged from the deep inner springs of the soul, our energies spread thinly across the surface of life with all its activities. We tend to "live in our heads," tightly binding our identity to who we *think* we are. Who we think we are is largely shaped by the archetypal self-images trumpeted by our culture: superficial pictures of womanhood and manhood; seductive images of power, control, possession, and self-indulgence; the false notion that we *are* what we *do*, especially what we achieve and produce. Images imposed on us by others' worldviews, values, wounded personalities, and life patterns also influence who we think we are. Both compliance with and rebellion against these influences shapes our sense of self, for even in rebellion our self-image is shaped by that against which we rebel! Who we think we are, then, is a complex web of images formed and fed largely by distorting influences. This structure of distorted identity is what we mean by the "false self."

We tend to associate our selfhood with the thoughts and feelings that arise from the process of our identity formation. These thoughts and feelings become norms by which we understand ourselves and engage the world around us. Our thoughts and feelings resemble an ever-changing kaleidoscope, coloring every situation with what we believe is our identity. So our sense of being becomes inseparable from the constant flux of our thoughts and feelings. We perceive the idea of silencing thoughts and feelings as a threat to our identity, even to our very existence!

American psychologist and philosopher, William James, alerts us to a different frame for seeking our identity, another possible source for our sense of self: "Our normal waking consciousness, rational consciousness as we call it, is but one special type of consciousness, whilst all about it, parted from it by the filmiest of screens, there lie potential forms of consciousness entirely different."[2]

We can think of *contemplatio* as an alternate form of consciousness, one that offers us a different way to discover our identity from

2. William James, *The Varieties of Religious Experience: A Study in Human Nature* (New York: New American Library, 1958), 298.

the false, exterior sense of self that is limited to our thoughts and feelings. Again, Merton counsels, "If we are involved only in our surface existence, in externals, and in the trivial concerns of our ego, we are untrue to [God] and to ourselves."[3]

In *contemplatio* we probably face the greatest hurdle to transformation in our scriptural encounters with God. The gift of salvation goes far beyond our capacity for rational thinking, and to receive the gift requires that at some point we move beyond our thoughts. In his prayer for the Ephesians that we studied in the last chapter, Paul includes a strange petition: that we come to "know the love of Christ which surpasses knowledge" (3:19). How can we know something that surpasses knowledge? This implies a mystery of deeper spiritual "knowing," a kind of intuitive, experiential knowledge that lies beyond our ordinary thinking and feeling. *Contemplatio* calls us to this way of knowing.

The stillness and silence of *contemplatio* has its earliest witness in scripture. A powerful biblical image of this way of being is found in Psalm 131: "Truly I have set my soul in silence and in peace, like a weaned child at its mother's breast, like a weaned child is my soul" (v. 2). The power of this image lies in the word *weaned*. An unweaned child is generally at its mother's breast for what it needs and wants—milk. Hunger and need drive the relationship to the point where the mother may feel she is hardly more than a human milk bottle! Of course, emotional nurture is given with physical nourishment, and the infant seeks comfort along with food.

The *weaned* child, however, relates to the mother in a different way. The "weaned child at its mother's breast" presents an image of the child's relaxed abandon in its mother's arms, of complete receptivity and trust, of allowing the mother to lavish her love upon the child in whatever way she chooses. It depicts the child simply being with and resting entirely upon its mother. In a sense, the image is that of the child's becoming "one" with the mother—not physically

In contemplative prayer the Spirit places us in a position where we are at rest and disinclined to fight.

—Thomas Keating

---

3. Thomas Merton, *Contemplation in a World of Action* (Notre Dame, IN: University of Notre Dame Press, 1998), 157.

but in deep relational bonding. The psalmist clearly intends the image to represent our spiritual relationship with God: "like a weaned child is my soul." In *contemplatio* we become the weaned child at its mother's breast.

The silence of *contemplatio* means stilling the maelstrom of our thoughts and feelings, which both reflect and reinforce our false identity. When our very sense of *being* has become inseparable from thoughts and feelings, the idea of stilling thoughts and feelings may threaten our existence. Perhaps this is why Jesus repeats, "If any would come after me, let them deny themselves, take up their cross and follow me" (see Matt. 16:24 and parallels). What does Jesus mean by denying the self? I do not believe he is talking about giving up candy for Lent! Jesus is calling us to abandon our false self, to relinquish our constructed identity with its supporting thoughts and feelings. This becomes clearer when Jesus calls us to take up our cross.

When we hear the word *cross*, we generally think of the crucifixion. We must remember that when Jesus' hearers heard this call, they had no idea Jesus was going to be crucified. In fact, Matthew 20:19 and 26:2 are the only Passion predictions in the Gospels that indicate Jesus will be crucified.[4] What, then, would the disciples have thought when they heard Jesus tell them to take up the cross? In the Roman world of the first century, the cross served as powerful symbol and notorious reality—an instrument of torture and execution that underscored the insignificance of the person being crucified. To be crucified was the ultimate experience of being dehumanized, marginalized, and degraded; it meant the total loss of a person's selfhood and identity. Thus the disciples would have heard Jesus telling them to abandon their very sense of identity, all that they knew of who they were.

The radical nature of Jesus' call becomes unmistakably clear in what he says next: "For those who want to save their life will lose it, and those who lose their life for my sake will find it" (Matt. 16:25). The identity shaped and reinforced by our thoughts and feelings per-

> *The purpose of contemplative prayer is to facilitate the process of inner transformation.*
>
> —Thomas Keating

---

4. Other Passion predictions simply indicate that Jesus will be killed—Matthew 16:21; 17:23; Mark 8:31; 9:31; 10:34; Luke 9:22; 18:33. We read "crucifixion" into these predictions after the fact, but the disciples are unlikely to have done so.

petually seeks to save itself. A false identity has to constantly protect itself against all threats, promote itself in a "dog-eat-dog" world, and root itself ever more firmly in the value system and behavior patterns of its deformed worldview. Yet on such a path, we lose sight of our true identity and risk losing it altogether.

Contemplatio calls us to abandon our false identity in order to discover our true identity that is "hid with Christ in God." Merton describes the losing and finding of true life this way:

> Thus in the highest sense the . . . contemplative life seems to be a sacrifice of identity, a "loss of the self," in order that there may be no self but that of God who is the object of our contemplation and of our praise. And this, paradoxically, is not self-alienation but the highest and most perfect "self-realization." . . .
>
> . . . The discipline involved here is that of a crucifixion which eliminates a superficial and selfish kind of experience and opens to us the freedom of a life that is not dominated by egoism, vanity, willfulness, passion, aggressiveness, jealousy, greed.[5]

The process of *lectio divina* may bring us into a divine encounter that simultaneously reveals to us something of God's true identity and something of our false identity. This is what I call the "Isaiah experience," based on the prophet's call in Isaiah 6:1-8. Isaiah, apparently a priest, has access to the sanctuary of the Temple. Presumably he is in the Temple performing his priestly duties. He is holy—that is, ritually pure—or he would not have dared enter the Temple. On this occasion, however, Isaiah encounters the living God. In that transforming encounter Isaiah also encounters himself: "'Woe is me! I am lost, for I am a man of unclean lips, and I live among a people of unclean lips; yet my eyes have seen the King, the Lord of hosts!'" (6:5). This cry is Isaiah's *oratio*, his heart's response to encountering God. We see Isaiah's *contemplatio* in his subsequent self-abandonment to God in the plea, "Here I am, send me!" (6:8).

In *contemplatio* we abandon our false and limited self to God. We also let go of false constructs we may call "God." We silence the noise of our false self in order simply to be. Like the weaned child, we

We have a giant obstacle in ourselves—our world view. It needs to be exchanged for the mind of Christ.

—Thomas Keating

---

5. Merton, *Contemplation in a World of Action*, 54–55, 113–114.

relinquish any agenda for what we want God to do and let the holy Mystery be with us as the Mystery chooses. In a real sense *contemplatio* signals a loss both of self and "God." We lose our world-shaped identity, which releases us to find our true self, hidden in the divine life. We also lose the "god" constructed by our false self to provide justification for our worldly identity. Our transformation by the Spirit into our true identity as persons fully bearing God's own image requires that we consistently relinquish "self" and let God be God in our life on divine terms, not human ones. This is precisely what *contemplatio* is about. In contemplation, the encounter with divine Mystery in the Word begins to transform us.

Perhaps we are wondering at this point how to practice *contemplatio*. We begin by learning the difficult discipline of becoming still. Here is a familiar but helpful exercise (it has circulated widely and is not original with me). We take the first part of Psalm 46:10 as our guide, and begin by repeating the entire phrase: "Be still, and know that I am God." We repeat it slowly several times, pausing each time and letting the "noise" of our surface identity fade into the background. Then we shorten the phrase to "Be still, and know that I am." Repeating this slowly several times, we pause each time and let the "noise" of our limited concept of "God" fade, letting "I am" be with us however "I am" chooses. Then we shorten the phrase again, "'Be still, and know.'" Repeating this slowly several times, we pause each time to be aware of "knowing" our very being enfolded and indwelt by "I am." We shorten the phrase yet again to "Be still." This too we repeat several times, pausing for longer periods of being still. Finally, we shorten the phrase to the single word "Be." Hopefully by this time we experience some small degree of abiding in God.

Another practice to assist us in becoming still involves taking a simple phrase and repeating it slowly, focusing on the reality it conveys. For instance, "I am a weaned child at its mother's breast," or "I am hid with Christ in God." A word or phrase from a passage with which you have been practicing *lectio divina* may express something of the quieter depths of your encounter with holy Mystery.

Contemplative prayer is a way of awakening to the reality in which we are immersed.

—Thomas Keating

Remember the context for contemplation: *silentio, lectio, meditatio, oratio* are all steps toward *contemplatio*. Each step builds toward transformation as we encounter God in the Word-become-text, but only in *contemplatio* is transformation fully released in us.

I want to sound two notes of caution as we close this chapter. First, if nothing seems to happen in *contemplatio*, we need not imagine we have failed or wasted our time. It is counterproductive to bring an agenda to this practice. Entering *contemplatio* with expectations undermines its purpose. Often when we say "nothing happened," we are really saying, "The Spirit didn't meet me as I expected." Yet the steady practice of *contemplatio*—seeking to sink down into the silence of God—is indeed working something in us. It nurtures us toward a more consistent yielding to God, fostering a deeper abiding in God.

Second, we have not completed the full process of *lectio divina* yet. The transforming dynamics of *contemplatio* find their fulfillment in the final step of *incarnatio*. Quaker writer Thomas Kelly describes the fruits of contemplation this way:

> We are torn loose from earthly attachments and ambitions—*contemptus mundi.*[6] And we are quickened to a divine but painful concern for the world—*amor mundi.*[7] [God] plucks the world out of our hearts, loosening the chains of attachment. And [God] hurls the world into our hearts, where we and [God] together carry it in infinitely tender love.[8]

It is to such *incarnatio* that we will turn in our final week.

---

6. "Contempt for the world"—a traditional monastic concept that rejects the deforming dynamics of worldliness.

7. "Love for the world"—meaning our participation in God's costly love for the world.

8. Thomas R. Kelly, *A Testament of Devotion* (San Francisco: HarperSanFrancisco, 1992), 19–20.

DAILY EXERCISES

Read Week 6, "*Contemplatio*: Abandoning Ourselves to God in Love." Note your insights, questions, and struggles. Journal with the exercises below, opening yourself to God's love with as much inner freedom and abandon as you can. Pray for grace to let go of your surface self and allow the indwelling Christ greater scope in your mind and heart.

EXERCISE 1

Read Ephesians 3:14-19. Come into God's presence. Read this prayer slowly, paying attention to the words or phrases that draw your spirit. Dwell in those phrases, allowing images, associations, and wonderings to arise. Let the Spirit speak to your heart. Let your heart respond. Capture the essence of this *lectio-meditatio-oratio* in your journal.

For a few minutes, ponder the phrase: to "know the love of Christ which surpasses knowledge." What does it mean to "know" beyond knowledge? What kind of knowing do you need to go beyond in order to know Christ? Seek this deeper, intuitive knowing. Then simply let yourself rest fully in Christ who knows you. Breathe in the fragrance; drink in the beauty; soak in the love of Christ.

EXERCISE 2

Read Isaiah 6:1-8. We refer to the prophet's vision of God in the Temple as "Isaiah's call." Our calls may be less dramatic, but the basic dynamics of the story ring true for us.

Identify with Isaiah's feeling of being "lost," living among people "of unclean lips." Imagine yourself standing before the throne of Majesty, surrounded by heavenly beings. What are you feeling? In your journal name your own "unclean lips" and those of the culture that has formed you.

As you ponder how your life needs to be purified and purged, what would be the equivalent of a "live coal" for you now? Draw a symbol or image of how God would meet you for healing and transformation. If ready, accept this image into your consciousness; let it free you for self-offering to God's service.

EXERCISE 3

Read Matthew 16:24-26. This teaching of Jesus expresses the crux of Christian discipleship, yet its familiarity can dull us to the radical sacrifice and freedom it signifies.

Focus on verse 25, the great paradox of faith. Chew on it awhile, praying for the Spirit to illumine its meaning. What is the life you want to "save"? What is the "life" you need to lose in order to find? What "self" needs to be denied in order to affirm your true identity? What greater self-interest is served by self-denial? Write a prayer or poem expressing your insights.

Allow yourself to be carried into a spirit of love for God.

EXERCISE 4

Read Exodus 3:1-6. In these verses that form the beginning of God's call to Moses, the Lord appears to him in a bush that burns but is not consumed.

Moses is tending sheep out "beyond the wilderness" when this extraordinary meeting occurs. His simple activity gives him plenty of time and space to notice unusual things. When have you known times or places of spaciousness in which you have recognized divine presence? Where, in the midst of ordinary life, have you met God in a deep way? Note your thoughts and memories.

These times and places in your life have been "holy ground." Choose to step onto holy ground right now, in prayer. Take off your shoes, find a posture of physical receptivity, and allow God to be with you as God chooses. Offer your listening presence to God, and pay attention to thoughts or feelings that may surface.

EXERCISE 5

Read Colossians 3:1-4. When we deny our surface self in order to free our true self in Christ, we begin to experience our life "hid with Christ in God."

Draw a line down the center of a journal page. On the left side, describe as fully as you can your "false self"—its fears, loves, cravings, defenses, envies, angers, and indiscretions. Write only what you know to be true about yourself, not the criticisms of others. On the right side, describe equally where you see your true self expressed and how Christlike characteristics are emerging: compassion, kindness, humility, patience, forgiveness, and love (see vv. 12-14).

Visualize your false self shrinking and evaporating, dying from lack of feeding. Confirm that you desire and choose this to happen in your daily life. Then imagine the heart of your true self held close to Jesus' heart, beating in rhythm with his, hidden together inside the cosmic heart of God. Feel the lifeblood of Love pulsing through you both in complete harmony. Carry this image with you into your day or evening with gratitude, and pray for its realization in your life.

Review the week's journal entries in preparation for the group meeting.

Week 7
Incarnatio: The Word Becoming Flesh in Us

W hatever light you then receive should be used to the uttermost, and that immediately. Let there be no delay. Whatever you resolve, begin to execute the first moment you can."[1] In these concluding instructions on reading the Bible, John Wesley affirmed in his own way the working assumptions I proposed as we began this journey: that the Word-become-text offers a transforming encounter with God so that the Word might become flesh in us. The divine purpose for us is Christlikeness. As *contemplatio* nurtures our intimacy with God, helping us grow into loving union with our Creator, Christ's love becomes increasingly visible in our lives. This is the meaning of *incarnatio*. The outcome of a deepening relationship with God is a life in which divine presence is ever more fully touching the lives of others in healing, freeing, transforming love.

Lectio *is founded in a Christian theology that takes the principle of incarnation quite seriously.*

—Norvene Vest

One way to understand *incarnatio* is to become sensitive to the difference between "being in the world for God" and "being in God for the world." For too many believers, the Christian life is about being in the world for God. Their lives are guided by a set of rules—dos and don'ts—that they believe will be acceptable and pleasing to God. They engage in various activities they think will gain God's approval and possibly affirmation from others. In God's name they attempt

---

1. Wesley, *Works of John Wesley*, 3rd ed., 14:253.

to impose their view of Christianity on those around them. The prob-lem is that *they* are in control. They obey rules and engage in reli-gious behaviors according to their own agenda. God is in their lives; but on their terms, not God's. They attempt to use God to make sure the world around them conforms to their ideals and purposes.

A rather disconcerting illustration of "being in the world for God" comes at the end of the Sermon on the Mount when Jesus says:

> It is not all those calling me "Lord, Lord," who will enter into the King-dom of Heaven, but those doing the will of my Father who is in heaven. Many will say to me in that day, "Lord, Lord, didn't we in your name prophesy; didn't we in your name drive out demons; and didn't we in your name do many powerful things?" And then I will say to them, "I never knew you! Get away from me you who are evil doing" (Matt. 7:21-23).[2]

Jesus is describing people who are in the world for God. They are clearly doing "God-things" and doing them "in Jesus' name." They seemingly epitomize those "doing the will of my Father who is in heaven." Surely activities like prophesying, driving out demons, and performing powerful deeds manifest holiness in the world. More-over, such activities clearly demonstrate that those doing them are God's people. In the words of Nicodemus, "No one is able to do these things unless God is with them" (John 3:2).

Jesus, however, relays a deeply disturbing word to these people: "I never knew you!" Their "God-things" are not the fruit of a vital relationship with Jesus. Their activities do not incarnate a life "hid with Christ in God." As a consequence, all their good works result in "evil doing"—not that the things they are doing are evil, but the *nature* of their doing is evil. Their "ministry" does not emerge from a rela-tionship of loving union with God, though they claim Jesus as Lord.

In John's Gospel, Jesus comes at this dimension of the Christian life from a different angle. He illustrates the nature of a person's rela-tionship with him through the image of a vine and its branches: "'Those who abide in me and I in them bear much fruit, because

---

2. My translation. In the Greek text, the phrase "in your name" introduces each activity, empha-sizing how convinced these people were that they were acting in Jesus' name.

apart from me you can do nothing'" (John 15:5). In our functionally oriented culture that confuses personal identity with what we do, this is probably the last saying of Jesus we will come to fully accept. For example, how many things have you already done today without any thought of Jesus? Note that Jesus does not say we *cannot* perform without him, only that *apart from him* our performance is nothing.

This is the great challenge and danger of *incarnatio*. We acknowledge that our encounter with God in the Word-become-text should make a difference in the way we live. So we set out to behave in a more "Christian" manner. We determine to engage in more "Christian" activities. We decide to become involved with the world in a more "Christian" way. Unless these behaviors emerge as a consequence of a deepening relationship of loving union with Christ, it is highly probable that we are simply being in the world for God.

The purpose of *lectio divina* is not to cloak us in a veneer of Christlikeness, an imitation *incarnatio*. The goal of *lectio divina* is the transformation of our being into actual Christlikeness. As the Word becomes flesh in us through our encounter with God in scripture, our transformed being moves into the world in a transforming way. We live the Christ-life by making real a profoundly changed perceptual framework and value system: "The purpose of our life is to bring all our strivings and desires into the sanctuary of the inner self and place them all under the command of an inner and God-inspired consciousness."[3] This is the meaning of "being in God for the world." To live in this way is *incarnatio*.

Incarnatio takes place in two arenas: the community of faith and the world. Paul provides several markers for how it is expressed in a body of believers. After exhorting the Ephesians to live a life worthy of their new calling,[4] Paul indicates that they are to do this "with all humility and gentleness, with long-suffering, forbearing one another in love, being zealous to maintain the unity of the Spirit in the bond

> *In* lectio *we are seeking to be transformed into Christ.*
>
> —Norvene Vest

---

3. Thomas Merton, *The Inner Experience: Notes on Contemplation*, ed. William H. Shannon (San Francisco: HarperSanFrancisco, 2003), 92.

4. Which, as we will see, is a life "of the full stature of Christ" (Eph. 4:13).

of peace" (Eph. 4:2-3). Humility, gentleness, patience, and forbearance are qualities of being that depend on finding our identity in God alone. As long as the archetypal self-images held up to us by our culture—superficial beauty or brawn, power and control, indulgence and possession, achievement and production—determine our identity, then our identity is set up over and against other people. Others become threats to our identity, objects to be manipulated to affirm our identity or persons upon whom our identity has become totally dependent. Under these distorting dynamics, what looks like humility may simply be a means to insure that the one on whom we depend for our identity will continue to allow our dependence. What appears as gentleness may be mere manipulation to affirm our identity by pacifying all threats to it. What seems to be long-suffering may be a way to avoid a menace to our identity.

Finding our identity in God alone frees us from these deceptive relational patterns. When we truly know ourselves in God, we can authentically embody Christlike humility, gentleness, patience, and forbearance so that they become a means of God's transforming presence in the lives of others.

Paul tells us these qualities of relationship are an expression of agape love. Since the essence of agape love is its radical focus on the well-being of others, loving this way shows an identity deeply rooted in God's love. *Contemplatio* enables us to experience such grounding in God.

Paul points us to this God-grounded identity when he speaks of "being zealous to maintain the unity of the Spirit in the bond of peace" (Eph. 4:3). The "unity of the Spirit" is the reality that prevails when two or more persons find their identity in God alone. Short of this, all unities are provisional. Consider the spokes of a wheel. On the rim of the wheel each spoke is an individual, separate from the rest of the spokes. At the hub of the wheel, however, all spokes become one in the hub. When a spoke becomes detached from the hub, it becomes eccentric (literally "out of the center"). A detached spoke threatens the integrity and well-being of the entire wheel. When spokes are one in the hub, however, they are bound together in a relationship of whole-

Interior silence is the perfect seed bed for divine love to take root.

—Thomas Keating

ness, integrity, and strength. *Incarnatio* in the community of faith seeks to realize this kind of profound unity in God.

Shortly after this passage, Paul tells us God has provided a variety of "offices"[5] in the community of faith for "training the saints for the work of ministry, for nurturing the body of Christ, until all come to the unity of the faith and of the knowledge of the Son of God, to maturity, to the measure of the stature of the fullness of Christ" (Eph. 4:12-13). Notice that the "work of ministry" is not the special gift of certain persons. The special gifts are for the "training of the saints." The saints (the whole Christian community) carry out the work of ministry, defined as "nurturing the body of Christ."[6] Paul describes this nurture with a double parallel structure:

$$\left[\begin{array}{l} \text{The unity of the faith } = \text{ knowledge of the Son of God} \\ \text{Maturity } = \text{ the measure of the stature of the fullness of Christ} \end{array} \right]$$

The "unity of the faith" Paul speaks of is that relationship of loving union with God which *contemplatio* nurtures and from which genuine *incarnatio* comes. This union is also a unity "of the knowledge of the Son of God." Remember that the term Paul uses for knowledge here describes experiential knowledge. It is relational knowing, the experience of life "hid with Christ in God." Relational knowing is not so much knowledge *about* as knowledge *of*. It is less a matter of right doctrinal beliefs than of intimate personal relationship in self-giving love. So the "unity of the faith" is a life joined with others in loving union with God, much like the unity of the spokes at the hub.

Paul defines this unity as "maturity." God created us for relationship of this quality; in it we find our true identity and through it we experience wholeness. Paul describes maturity as "the measure of the stature of the fullness of Christ." In other words, maturity is Christlikeness. Recall that the entire reason for the Word becoming

If you stay with lectio, *you will discover that you are growing more and more into the mind and heart of Christ.*

—Norvene Vest

---

5. Prophets, apostles, evangelists, pastor-teachers (4:11).

6. The Greek text is quite clear: that for which the saints are equipped is expressed in two mutually defining phrases: (1) the work of ministry, and (2) building up the body of Christ. These are two ways of saying the same thing. The work of ministry is building up the body of Christ.

text is to provide a place of transforming encounter with God so that the Word might become flesh in us. In the mutual relationship of loving union with God, we find our personal identity as Christlike beings and the body of believers becomes the body of Christ.

How do we implement *incarnatio* in the community of faith? We could devote an entire book to answering this question, but here are a few guidelines drawn from the epistles.

First, Paul tells us that "speaking the truth in love, we must grow up . . . into Christ" (Eph. 4:15). The crux here is "speaking the truth in love." Paul uses this same term in Galatians 4:16. There, in one of his harshest letters, he takes the Galatians to task for having turned away from the gospel of grace to works of the Law. At the same time, he seeks to restore them to the wholeness of life in Christ. Seemingly, "speaking the truth" is both a critique of living contrary to Christlikeness and an appeal to Christlikeness, individually and corporately. For this reason, "speaking the truth in love" is the means for "growing up in every way into him who is the head, into Christ." It is vital to see that the primary motive for this practice is agape love. Christian love is a posture of profound other-centeredness, a primary concern for the wholeness and well-being of the other—both for the individual and the community of faith.

Second, Paul provides a step-by-step process by which God's love can be incarnated within the community of faith. Writing to the Galatians, he counsels:

> If anyone is overtaken by any transgression, you who are spiritual restore such a one in a spirit of gentleness watching out for yourselves lest you also be tempted. Bear one another's burdens, and in this way you will fulfill the law of Christ (6:1-2).

Notice the steps Paul provides: First, he indicates "you who are spiritual." He is not talking about busybodies who pry into the lives of others. This is Paul's version of getting the log out of your own eye before messing with the speck in another's eye (Matt. 7:3-5). To be spiritual is to be the presence of Christ for others, to be abandoned to God in love for others, to hold the welfare of others as a primary value. Second, the purpose is to "restore such a one." Paul does not give license to condemn, judge, or demean a person who has gone off the road of Christlikeness. Restoration is the only goal. The purpose is to bring the person back to the path of life. Third, all is to be done "in a spirit of gentleness" or humility. There is no basis here for an attitude of superiority, self-righteousness, or condescension. Restoration is to be sought in a Christlike spirit. Finally, Paul enjoins us to "watch out for ourselves" lest we too get tempted. Tempted to do the same things as the one needing restoration? Perhaps, but more likely tempted to see ourselves as morally superior to the fallen brother or sister; or maybe tempted to manipulate them into our own narrow view of what it means to be Christian. In the likeness of Christ who bore the burden of our alienation from God, we are to incarnate that burden-bearing in our relationship with others, helping to restore their relationship with God and the faith community.

Incarnatio in the body of believers is nurturing one another to Christlikeness. For this purpose the Word became text to provide a place of transforming divine encounter.

Yet incarnation is not just for the community of faith. *Incarnatio* in the body of Christ is finally for the sake of the world. Individually it means being the presence of Christ for others in the world; corporately it means being the body of Christ in the world. Here is a collage of thoughts that may stimulate further ideas of how *incarnatio* plays out in the world through us.

- "God so loved the world" (John 3:16) makes incarnation in that world an essential dimension of relationship with God. Ancient Greek culture employed three meanings of "world": (1) the whole Cosmos, (2) the earth and its creatures, and (3) the negative sense of destructive powers and principalities. It could be valuable to ponder how God's love relates to each and how we might incarnate God's transforming love in relation to the second and third meanings of "world."

- Genuine *incarnatio* finds expression in every dimension of the world. As a paraphrase of John Wesley goes, there can be no personal holiness without social holiness. Since holiness is another

The word of God is then able to prove itself by its transforming power which brings love, unity, peace, understanding and freedom where before there were prejudice, conflict, hatred, division and greed.

—Thomas Merton

way of speaking of Christlikeness, there can be no personal Christ-likeness that is not in and for the world. How then might our personal prayer and corporate worship give expression to concern for right relationship, justice, forgiveness, and reconciliation?

- Author Kenneth Leech asks, "But what happens when theology becomes captured . . . by the prevailing culture? Theology . . . then becomes a resource of the culture, and no longer its critic. . . . The God of justice is tamed and put at the service of organized injustice."[7] Ponder where you have seen or heard of situations, before or during your lifetime, in which a living relationship with God has been squeezed into a rigid theology that serves cultural or political purposes. What would it mean to live the Christ-life in such a situation? How do you dream of practicing *incarnatio* in those uncomfortable situations that call for courage and change?

God invites us to share in the divine life, even as we go about our everyday activities!

—Norvene Vest

- *Incarnatio* flings us into the world to live out our relationship of loving union with God. Entering scripture as a place of transforming encounter with God, we discover a gospel that is not harmonious with the values of prevailing ideologies, inside or outside the church. The Word-become-text challenges our worldly views, values, and behaviors—personally and corporately. How will *incarnatio* call us to resist worldly indoctrination and become, with Christ, the Word-made-flesh for the world?

- *Incarnatio* is the intrusion of God's reign in the world. It reveals to the world an alternative to destructive dynamics, bringing divine life into the deadness of the world, light into its darkness, forgiveness to its sinfulness, healing to its woundedness, wholeness to its brokenness, and liberating power to its bondage. *Incarnatio* has at its heart cruciform love. Those whose position, power, and prestige are grounded in the dehumanizing views, values, and behaviors of the world will take action to eliminate any threats to that world. *Incarnatio* may well result in some version of crucifixion.

---

7. Kenneth Leech, *Experiencing God: Theology as Spirituality* (San Francisco: Harper and Row, 1985), 384.

What inner motivation and strength do we bring to the very real likelihood of such suffering?

• To be an authentic disciple of Jesus means to stand with him as a sign of contradiction to worldly values and judgments. The power of the gospel helps us determine thoughts, sources of inspiration, and models of life that are in keeping with the Word of God and the gift of salvation. What persons of faith, present or past, best embody this *incarnatio* in your view? What stories could you tell?

Whatever perspectives you may have started with seven weeks ago, my prayer is that through reading, reflection, prayer, and the practice of *lectio divina* in your *Companions* group, the scriptures have increasingly become a place of transforming encounter with God for you, as they have been for me these many decades. I pray that your continued encounters with the Word-become-text will lead you to abandon yourself to God in love more and more freely so that this Word may truly "become flesh" again in your life—for the sake of a church and world that need desperately to experience the reality and beauty of Christ in his followers. May God give you grace to bear such witness with joy!

In the frequent use of Scripture, a person goes on discovering it progressively, and this process never ends.

—García M. Colombás

DAILY EXERCISES

Read Week 7, "*Incarnatio*: The Word Becoming Flesh in Us." Note your insights and interior movements. Journal with these daily exercises, seeking clarity about the ways you do and can incarnate the love of Christ in this world. Give particular attention to exercises 4 and 5, with special focus on the segments marked with a star.* This will be important to your group meeting process in this final week together. Pray for grace and courage to give God's love full rein in your inward and outward daily life.

EXERCISE 1

Read John 15:4-13. In Week 2 we explored this passage through the lens of abiding in Christ as a way of being. We revisit it now from the angle of fruitfulness. As you read, notice how the term *abiding* relates to bearing fruit.

Ponder how dwelling or remaining in Christ and his Word leads to fruitfulness. The core "words" of Jesus that live in us as we dwell in him are found in verses 12-13. Reflect on how the command to love as Jesus has loved us can make our joy complete.

Breathe in Christ's love for you. Soak it into your soul. Then begin prayerfully to breathe it out in prayer for others who have need of that love. Let the Spirit bring to mind those who need your love. After a time, invite God to help you see ways to love these people more fully in your encounters and interactions with them. Record insights.

EXERCISE 2

Read John 8:31-36. Jesus invites those who believe in him to "'continue in my word'" (NRSV) so they might taste the freedom from sin that comes from knowing the truth—truth Jesus himself embodies.

Dwell awhile on the phrase "'you will know the truth, and the truth will make you free'" (v. 32, NRSV). There are two basic kinds of freedom: freedom *from* and freedom *for*. Write these two categories at the top of a journal page with a line drawn down the middle. Reflect in each column: What do you need to be set free *from*? What do you wish to be free *for*? Ask yourself how these freedoms connect; draw lines or arrows between the columns indicating connections you see. Let your reflections carry you into prayer. Allow yourself to use posture, gestures, and movement to express what you yearn to be released from and what you desire to give yourself to. Then take a moment to listen for what your body may be teaching you about prayer.

EXERCISE 3

Read John 10:31-38. Jesus has done many "great works" from God that witness to his identity. He basically says, "Don't take my word for who I am, judge me by the fruits you see" and "Believe the works, so that you may know and understand who I am."

What works do you believe God wants to accomplish through you? Can you identify a creative, healing, or encouraging <u>work</u> of God in your own soul that wants to find expression in this world? When others observe or interact with you, what spiritual fruit do you hope they will see or experience? How will others know you belong to God in Christ? Journal with any of these questions that draw you.

Recall that any lasting significance of your works comes out of loving union with Christ. Take time to root yourself in God through prayer, asking the Spirit to guide and prosper your works as an expression of your deep identity in Christ.

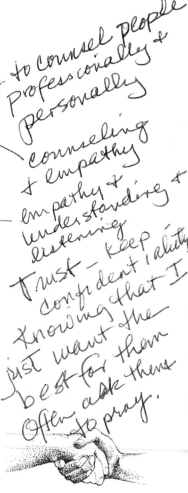

to counsel people professionally & personally

counseling & empathy

empathy & understanding listening

Trust — keep confidentiality knowing that I just want the best for them

Often ask them to pray.

EXERCISE 4

Read Ephesians 4:11-16 and 4:25–5:2. Our author feels strongly that unity of faith, knowledge of Christ, and spiritual maturity are all one cloth. Verses 4:25–5:2 paint a picture of a mature life in Christ.

Reflect on the idea of maturity in Christ. What does it look like? List in your journal some character traits you would identify with Christlikeness. Where have you experienced such maturity in yourself or in others you know?

*Write a brief (one- to two-paragraph) story or incident describing someone you consider to be mature in Christ. What inspiration do you take from this person? Be prepared to share this story at your final weekly meeting.

EXERCISE 5

Read Mark 14:3-9. We spent time with this passage in Week 3, entering the story with our senses and imagination. Revisit it now, focusing on the "good service" Jesus says this woman performs for him, anointing his body for burial.

Reflect on why the woman's lavish act was indeed a good service rather than a waste of expensive ointment. A paraphrase of Jesus words might be, "She has done a beautiful thing for me." What beautiful work are you called to do for Christ? What "fragrance" would you want people to remember you by? Note thoughts in your journal.

*Now take time to review the scripture passages that have spoken most deeply to you over the course of these seven weeks. Which one or two especially bear the marks of a call, the sense of a new claim on your life? How will you embody this call in your life? Make an act of interior commitment to God in prayer. Then find or create a small token (symbol) of your commitment to take with you to the final group meeting.

Review the week's journal entries in preparation for the group meeting.

An Annotated Resource List from Upper Room Ministries

*T*he following list contains information about books in the Companions in Christ series, and other books that expand on the subject matter of *The Way of Scripture*. The Upper Room has published all the books listed; the number in parentheses is the ISBN number to give when ordering by phone or online. Order these books online at www.upperroom.org/bookstore or by calling 1-800-972-0433.

THE COMPANIONS IN CHRIST SERIES

Companions in Christ: A Small-Group Experience in Spiritual Formation (Participant's Book, #978-0-8358-9843-0) by Stephen D. Bryant, Gerrit Scott Dawson, Adele J. Gonzalez, E. Glenn Hinson, Rueben P. Job, Marjorie J. Thompson, and Wendy M. Wright

Companions in Christ: A Small Group Experience in Spiritual Formation (Leader's Guide, #978-0-8358-9840-9) by Marjorie J. Thompson and Stephen D. Bryant

Twenty-eight weeks of readings and exercises from well-known authors guide participants into a richer experience of God. The five parts of *Companions in Christ* include: Embracing the Journey (spiritual formation as a journey toward wholeness and holiness); Feeding on the Word (reading scripture in fresh ways); Deepening Our Prayer (various forms and styles of prayer); Responding to Our Call (serving God in willing obedience); and Exploring Spiritual Guidance (ways of giving and receiving spiritual guidance). Each part offers spiritual practices to help sustain a lifelong faith journey.

The Leader's Guide provides detailed outlines and material for leading each of the weekly meetings. It also helps the leader identify and develop leadership qualities called upon when leading formational groups—qualities such as patience, trust, acceptance, and holy listening skills. The rich content brings a unique experience to each of the twenty-eight weeks.

Companions in Christ: The Way of Blessedness (Participant's Book, #978-0-8358-0992-4) by Stephen D. Bryant and Marjorie J. Thompson

Companions in Christ: The Way of Blessedness (Leader's Guide) by Stephen D. Bryant (#978-0-8358-0994-8)
The Way of Blessedness invites small group members to discover and live in the kingdom of God. Each week participants explore one of the Beatitudes from the Sermon on the Mount. The nine-week journey into Matthew 5 leads us through spiritual practices that help fill us with the love of God and love for the human family.

Companions in Christ: The Way of Discernment (Participant's Book, #978-0-8358-9958-1) by Stephen V. Doughty with Marjorie J. Thompson

Companions in Christ: The Way of Discernment (Leader's Guide, #978-0-8358-9959-8) by Marjorie J. Thompson
The Way of Discernment focuses on the ancient spiritual discipline of discernment for the individual, congregations, or larger bodies of the church. This ten-week study leads to the prayerful path of a richer, wiser life both for individuals and the larger church.

Companions in Christ: The Way of Forgiveness (Participant's Book, #978-0-8358-0980-1) by Marjorie J. Thompson

Companions in Christ: The Way of Forgiveness (Leader's Guide, #978-0-8358-0981-8) by Stephen D. Bryant and Marjorie J. Thompson
The Way of Forgiveness uses scripture meditation and other spiritual practices to guide us through an eight-week exploration of the forgiven and forgiving life. Always keeping God's grace and our blessedness before us, we examine shame, guilt, and anger before turning to forgiveness and reconciliation.

Companions in Christ: The Way of Grace (Participant's Book, #978-0-8358-9878-2) by John Indermark

Companions in Christ: The Way of Grace (Leader's Guide, #978-0-8358-9879-9) by Marjorie J. Thompson and Melissa Tidwell
The Way of Grace is a nine-week resource that provides a fresh approach to the Gospel of John. It invites us to travel with eight biblical characters who discover God's grace through their encounter with Jesus.

Companions in Christ: The Way of Prayer (Participant's Book, #978-0-8358-9906-2) by Jane Vennard

Companions in Christ: The Way of Prayer (Leader's Guide, #978-0-8358-9907-9) by Marjorie J. Thompson
The Way of Prayer is a ten-week resource designed to help people expand their understanding of the nature and practice of prayer. Participants with different temperaments, spiritual types, and learning styles will find expressions of prayer that draw them closer to God.

Companions in Christ: The Way of Transforming Discipleship (Participant's Book, #978-0-8358-9842-3) by Trevor D. Hudson and Stephen D. Bryant

Companions in Christ: The Way of Transforming Discipleship (Leader's Guide, #978-0-8358-9841-6) by Stephen D. Bryant
The Way of Transforming Discipleship, a five-week resource, challenges Christians to live the whole gospel by connecting spirituality with discipleship. A vital transformation begins when we know who we are, change from the inside out, listen to the groans of others, and discover the deep spirituality of belonging.

Exploring the Way: An Introduction to the Spiritual Journey (Participant's Book, #978-0-8358-9806-5) by Marjorie J. Thompson

Exploring the Way: An Introduction to the Spiritual Journey (Leader's Guide, #978-0-8358-9807-2) by Marjorie J. Thompson And Stephen D. Bryant

Exploring the Way, a six-week study, was created with those new to spiritual formation in mind. Intended to graciously introduce participants to basic spiritual practice, this book serves as an ideal introduction to the Companions in Christ series.

The Upper Room Worshipbook (#978-0-8358-9874-4), a rich collection of hymns, liturgies, psalm settings, global songs, and prayer, is an essential resource for individuals or congregations.

OTHER BOOKS OF INTEREST

Dimensions of Prayer: Cultivating a Relationship with God (#978-0-8358-0971-9, paperback) by Douglas V. Steere
In a rereleased version of his classic book, Steere answers common questions and concerns about prayer. This easy-to-read book offers new pray-ers an engaging introduction to prayer while providing valuable wisdom for mature Christians.

Gathered in the Word: Praying the Scripture in Small Groups (#978-0-8358-0806-4) by Norvene Vest
For those thirsting for God, Vest describes *lectio divina,* an age-old form of devotional reading that is intended specifically for spiritual nourishment.

A Guide to Prayer for All Who Seek God (#978-0-8358-1001-2, paperback) by Rueben P. Job and Norman Shawchuck
A marvelous gift book for friends, family, or even oneself, this book offers daily guidance. Each day's reading presents an opening affirmation, a petition of prayer and a scripture selection. Themed "Readings for Reflection" include excerpts from writers such as Frederick Buechner, Mother Teresa, Howard Thurman, C. S. Lewis, Dietrich Bonhoeffer, and John Wesley.

Questions God Asks Us (#978-0-8358-9990-1) by Trevor Hudson
Many people think of the Bible as a book of answers, but Hudson sees it as a book of questions: from God to us. God wants to enter into a conversational relationship with each person. So God poses questions, and our answers draw us into a deeper intimacy with God.

There are five questions from the Old Testament and five from the New Testament.

Shaped by the Word: The Power of Scripture in Spiritual Formation (#978-0-8358-0936-8) by M. Robert Mulholland
Mulholland examines obstacles we often encounter in spiritual reading and introduces a way of study that enlivens the scriptures. He demonstrates how our approach to scripture often determines its transforming effect upon our lives. An ideal resource for examining daily patterns of attentiveness to God.

The Upper Room Dictionary of Christian Spiritual Formation (#978-0-8358-0993-1) edited by Keith Beasley-Topliffe
When you need practical information about spiritual formation, *The Upper Room Dictionary of Christian Spiritual Formation* is an essential and basic resource. Nearly five hundred articles cover the people, methods, and concepts associated with spiritual formation, emphasizing prayer and other spiritual disciplines.

THE MEETING GOD IN SCRIPTURE SERIES
SMALL-GROUP RESOURCES

Entering the Old Testament, Participant's Workbook (#978-0-8358-9945-1)

Entering the Old Testament, Leader's Guide (#978-0-8358-9946-8)

Be still, toss aside your preconceptions, and immerse yourself in formative readings from Genesis to the Latter Prophets. Entering the Old Testament is an eight-week survey comprised of forty short readings that testify to the fact that even in the midst of struggle, we can commune with God and be transformed.

Entering the New Testament, Participant's Workbook (#978-0-8358-9967-3)

Entering the New Testament, Leader's Guide (#978-0-8358-9968-0)

Introduce your small-group participants to a rich way of reading New Testament scripture—the classic spiritual practice of praying with scripture. 8 weeks.

Entering the Psalms, Participant's Workbook (#978-0-8358-9973-4)

Entering the Psalms, Leader's Guide (#978-0-8358-9975-8)

Entering the Psalms models the movement from reading scripture to personal prayer, using entry-point questions to deepen the participant's engagement with scripture. 6 weeks.

Understanding Spiritual Gifts, Participant's Workbook (#978-0-8358-1015-9)

Understanding Spiritual Gifts, Leader's Guide (#978-0-8358-1014-2)

Identify your spiritual gifts and those of your congregation. Discover how God wants you to use each spiritual gift. Includes a spiritual gifts inventory. 7 weeks.

The Meeting God Bible: Growing in Intimacy with God through Scripture (#978-0-8358-9980-2, hardcover, NRSV)

The Meeting God Bible (NRSV) is an excellent addition to your individual or small-group study and reflection time. Designed to engage spirit, mind, and heart, this unique Bible helps turn scripture reading into a transforming encounter with God. Over 1,500 entry-point reflections help readers tap into the vital heart of scripture through time-tested spiritual disciplines. This Bible, previously published as *The Spiritual Formation Bible*, makes an excellent gift.

OTHER SMALL-GROUP RESOURCES

Do What You Have the Power to Do: Studies of Six New Testament Women (#978-0-8358-0643-5) by Helen Bruch Pearson
Pearson brings us face-to-face with empowering stories of New Testament women to help us create a clearer vision of Jesus in our lives.

Holy Adventure: 41 Days of Audacious Living (#978-0-8358-9970-3) by Bruce G. Epperly
Forty-one days of progressive spiritual guidance invites us into the challenge, the risk, and the uncertainty of the Christian journey that leads to a meaningful relationship with God.

Hope: Our Longing for Home (#978-0-8358-9921-5) by John Indermark
Authentic hope involves action, and action requires you to make choices. Indermark invites group members to be formed by true hope—a journey not only toward God but with God. 9 weeks—Leader's Guide included.

The Power of a Focused Heart: 8 Life Lessons from the Beatitudes (#978-0-8358-9818-8) by Mary Lou Redding
This book uses the Beatitudes as guides for simplifying life and setting spiritually based priorities. Brief chapters are followed by daily exercises in responding to scripture.

The Workbook on Abiding in Christ: The Way of Living Prayer (#978-0-8358-1028-9) by Maxie Dunnam.
Building upon the foundation of *The Workbook of Living Prayer* (but not a prerequisite for this workbook), *The Workbook on Abiding in Christ* "is not simply a study; it is a spiritual journey." This workbook contains 8 weeks of daily exercises and full group sessions for each of those eight weeks.

Sources and Authors of Margin Quotations

WEEK 1 SCRIPTURE: A PLACE OF TRANSFORMING ENCOUNTER

Stephen E. Fowl and L. Gregory Jones, *Reading in Communion: Scripture and Ethics in Christian Life* (Grand Rapids, MI: William B. Eerdmans Publishing Company, 1991), 30.

Fowl and Jones, *Reading in Communion*, 140–41.

Fowl and Jones, *Reading in Communion*, 145.

Irenaeus of Lyons, 2nd century.

García M. Colombás, *Reading God*, trans. Gregory J. Roettger (Schuyler, NE: Benedictine Mission House Publications, 1993), 68.

WEEK 2 *SILENTIO*: PREPARING TO BE READ BY SCRIPTURE

Colombás, *Reading God*, 17.

Thomas Merton, *Opening the Bible* (Collegeville, MN: Liturgical Press, 1970), 17.

Daniel Wolpert, *Creating a Life with God: The Call of Ancient Prayer Practices* (Nashville, TN: Upper Room Books, 2003), 40.

Wolpert, *Creating a Life with God*, 29.

E. Herman, *Creative Prayer* (Cincinnati, OH: Forward Movement Publication, n.d.), 40.

Norvene Vest, *No Moment Too Small: Rhythms of Silence, Prayer, and Holy Reading* (Kalamazoo, MI: Cistercian Publications; Boston: Cowley Publications, 1994), 26.

Dietrich Bonhoeffer, *Life Together*, trans. John W. Doberstein (New York: Harper and Row, Publishers, 1976), 79.

Norvene Vest, *Gathered in the Word: Praying the Scripture in Small Groups* (Nashville, TN: Upper Room Books, 1996), 41.

WEEK 3 *LECTIO*: INGESTING THE WORD

Marjorie J. Thompson, *Soul Feast: An Invitation to the Christian Spiritual Life* (Louisville, KY: Westminster John Knox Press, 1995), 21.

Wolpert, *Creating a Life with God*, 39.

Wolpert, *Creating a Life with God*, 41.

Richard J. Foster, *Prayer: Finding the Heart's True Home* (San Francisco: HarperSanFrancisco, 1992), 150.

Foster, *Prayer*, 147.

Colombás, *Reading God*, 42.

Colombás, *Reading God*, 43.

WEEK 4 *MEDITATIO*: WRESTLING WITH GOD

Foster, *Prayer*, 146.

Colombás, *Reading God*, 41.

Ibid., 90.

Bonhoeffer, *Life Together*, 81–82.

Vest, *Gathered in the Word*, 39.

Bonhoeffer, *Life Together*, 83.

Gregory the Great, c. 540–604.

Marchiene Vroon Rienstra, *Come to the Feast: Seeking God's Bounty for Our Lives and Souls* (Grand Rapids, MI: William B. Eerdman's Publishing Company, 1995), 20.

WEEK 5 *ORATIO*: LETTING GOD KNOW HOW WE FEEL

Ron DelBene, *The Breath of Life Workbook* (Nashville, TN: Upper Room Books, 1996), 46.

Bonhoeffer, *Life Together*, 84–85.

Arnold of Bohéries, 12th century.

Thompson, *Soul Feast*, 24.

Colombás, *Reading God*, 89.

WEEK 6 *CONTEMPLATIO*: ABANDONING OURSELVES TO GOD IN LOVE

Thompson, *Soul Feast*, 24.

Thomas Keating, *Open Mind, Open Heart: The Contemplative Dimension of the Gospel* (Rockport, MA: Element, 1992), 45.

Ibid., 45.

Ibid.

Ibid., 44.

WEEK 7 *INCARNATIO*: THE WORD BECOMING FLESH IN US

Vest, *Gathered in the Word*, 30.

Ibid., 34.

Keating, *Open Mind, Open Heart*, 45.

Vest, *No Moment Too Small*, 66.

Merton, *Opening the Bible*, 11.

Vest, *Gathered in the Word*, 30.

Colombás, *Reading God*, 66.

About the Authors

Dr. M. Robert Mulholland Jr. is professor emeritus of New Testament at Asbury Theological Seminary where he taught for thirty-one years and is a retired elder in the Kentucky Annual Conference of the United Methodist Church. He has been a faculty presenter for both two-year and five-day Academies for Spiritual Formation since the inception of the Academy movement in 1983 and has been a member of the Advisory Board of the Academy since 2000. Dr. Mulholland has authored *Shaped by the Word: The Role of Scripture in Spiritual Formation* (Upper Room), *Invitation to a Journey: A Roadmap of Spiritual Formation* (InterVarsity Press), and *The Deeper Journey: The Spirituality of Discovering Your True Self* (InterVarsity Press), and is a consulting editor for the *Journal of Spiritual Formation and Soul Care*.

Marjorie J. Thompson has worked closely with all facets of *Companions in Christ* from its origins and has helped guide and shape this small-group ministry for more than a decade. She brings to her ministry over twenty-five years of experience in retreat work, teaching, and writing in the area of Christian spiritual formation. For twelve years she served as director of Pathways in Congregational Spirituality with Upper Room Ministries. The author of *Soul Feast: An Invitation to the Christian Spiritual Life* (Westminster/John Knox Press, 1995/2005) and *Family, the Forming Center* (Upper Room Books, 1989/1996), she considers writing a central dimension of her calling as an ordained minister in the Presbyterian Church (USA).